Meet the Iguana

- Most iguanas are not trainable.

- Iguanas are cold-blooded and depend on temperatures ranging between 85° to 100°F to regulate their internal temperature.

- Iguanas need to be in direct sunlight (or underneath an artificial ultraviolet light) as much as possible.

- Because they spend so much time in the heat and sun, iguanas need a lot of water to keep their skin and bodies hydrated.

- Iguanas are called folivores—leaf-eating animals. Their diets consist of plant material and some fruit. Iguanas are very exacting in their dietary requirements, and severe health problems can result from an improper diet.

- "Iguana" is the interpretation Spanish explorers gave to the name the native American Caribbean Indians called these lizards, which was *iwana*.

- Iguanas grow quickly and get very large. Within a few years, that cute little hatchling in the pet store will be 5 or 6 feet long and will require spacious accommodations.

- Iguanas have long life spans. Captive iguanas have lived as long as twenty-five years.

- Most iguanas have tails that grow to two to three times their actual body length. All iguanas shed their skin.

Consulting Editor
LENNY FLANK, JR.

Featuring Photographs by
ZIG LESZCZYNSKI

Howell Book House
An Imprint of Macmillan General Reference USA
A Pearson Education Macmillan Company
1633 Broadway
New York, NY 10019-6785

Library of Congress Cataloging-in-Publication Data
The essential iguana/ consulting editor, Lenny Flank, Jr.; featuring photographs by Zig Leszczynski.
        p. cm.
Includes bibliographical references and index.
ISBN 1-58245-079-X
1. Green iguanas as pets.   I. Flank, Lenny.   II. Leszczynski, Zig.
SF459.I38E77   1999   98-53979
639.3'95—dc21   CIP

Manufactured in the United States of America
10 9 8 7 6 5 4 3 2

Series Director: Michele Matrisciani
Production Team: Carrie Allen, Heather Pope and
    Christina Van Camp
Book Design: Paul Costello
Photography: All photos by Zig Leszczynski.

ARE YOU READY?!

☐ Have you prepared your home and your family for your new pet?

☐ Have you gotten the proper supplies you'll need to care for your iguana?

☐ Have you found a veterinarian who is experienced in treating reptiles?

☐ Have you educated yourself about the iguana's behavior and personality?

☐ Have you taught your children and friends the proper way to hold your iguana?

No matter what stage you're at with your iguana—still thinking about getting one, or it's already part of the family—this Essential guide will provide you with the practical information you need to understand and care for your reptile companion. Of course you're ready—you have this book!

Iguana

SIGHT

Iguanas have excellent color vision. Like all arboreal animals, they are very good at judging distances. Iguanas also have a pineal gland. Located at the top of the head, this gland is also known as the "third eye." It is used to sense patterns of light and dark.

SOUND

Iguanas have very good hearing. They are sensitive to many frequencies that are undetectable by humans.

TASTE

An iguana uses its tongue as a way of providing information about its surroundings. Scent and taste particles are picked up on the tongue and transferred to a sensitive area in the roof of the mouth called the Jacobson's organ.

TOUCH

Although the iguana's skin has nerve endings to sense temperature, they are not very sensitive, particularly in the belly region.

SMELL

Iguanas smell with their tongues. They pick up scent molecules in the air and transfer them to the Jacobson's organ in the roof of their mouth. You will see your iguana periodically "taste-testing" things with its tongue as it picks up scent information.

CHAPTER ONE

Getting to Know Your Iguana

An iguana is not a puppy or a kitten or a hamster. Therefore, it cannot be treated like one. Normal household activity may be fine for the new puppy but is definitely not for the iguana. The iguana is naturally very suspicious toward other animals, human or otherwise, basically because it is concerned with its own safety. If you scare it with rough-and-tumble tactics, your iguana will become aggressive, and both of you can get hurt.

If you don't want your iguana to be afraid of you, then be gentle, calm, slow and steady in your movements. No quick movements! No running around! No throwing the iguana up in the air! No shouting, screaming or blaring stereos! Gentle, slow and quiet are the key words in any iguana's happy, healthy life.

The iguana is a solitary creature and needs to be slowly and gently introduced to people and other animals.

GAINING THE IGUANA'S TRUST

Ironically, the most important way to gain the trust of your iguana is to give it a little privacy. Providing it with a place where it can go to be alone will fulfill your pet's instinctual need to have its own space. Iguanas are very territorial. They live in small groups in which a single adult male gathers a small harem of mature females. Males defend their territory aggressively from each other. Females also squabble with each other to establish a dominance hierarchy. Iguanas are truly happier alone, even preferring to live away from other iguanas. No matter what your desires may be, there are times when iguanas need to be by themselves, and you must respect those feelings if you are to have an enduring relationship. Once an iguana feels comfortable with its surroundings, it will start to trust you, and that's when the real fun begins.

READING BODY LANGUAGE

The very cautious nature of an iguana is borne out by studying the animal's posture and positioning. By understanding this, you can gain insight into what the iguana is thinking. Is it afraid? Does it run away every time you enter the room, or does it move slowly and with confidence? Does it sit there, unmoving? You must learn to read its body language as a way of communication. Its movement will tell you how it is feeling and what its mood is.

A NEW KIND OF PET

Iguanas, by nature, are not very social animals. Don't handle your iguana too often immediately after you have obtained it. Some physical contact is important, but don't smother it with affection.

Iguanas' behavior can range from reserved to aggressive to comical when they are confident of their surroundings. If you provide safety and a sense of calm, and if you are patient and give your iguana enough time to be alone, you will enjoy a healthy pet.

It is very important that you understand that even if you do everything correctly and give your pet its own space and time to be alone, there are going to be periods where your iguana is upset, nervous, excited or aggressive. Don't panic; you didn't fail. Give your iguana more space and start over again slowly and patiently.

HOW THE IGUANA SEES THINGS

In the wild, iguanas form small solitary groups, living a quiet life, rarely interacting with other animals. The

3

The safer the iguana feels, the less timid its behavior.

*Iguanas inter-
pret loud sounds
and quick move-
ments as preda-
tory threats.*

4

iguana would be more than happy to be alone most of its life. In fact, it is best to have only one pet iguana per enclosure. It's not that the iguana wants no contact with human beings; it is just that sometimes we want too much. The iguana lives its life in fear until otherwise convinced that you mean no harm. That's why it's important to provide the iguana with trust. Handling comes much later. When your iguana is scared or afraid, do not try to handle or pet it. This only increases its fear.

Loud noises and sudden actions are absolute no-nos. Iguanas may interpret these noises or movements as threats or violence. And no parties! The iguana does not make for a good college fraternity mascot. Keep your pet in an area that is quiet and undisturbed.

In addition, do not make any harsh sounds in front of your iguana. Don't make loud noises or bark, meow, squeal or hiss—or anything your pet might construe as hostile or predatory.

WHAT TO DO WITH A DIFFICULT IGUANA

If your iguana is not responding to your patient attempts at interaction, don't get depressed. The first thing to do is to carefully examine the environment from your iguana's point of view.

- Is there another pet in the house that is intruding in your iguana's space?

- Is the aquarium or cage too close to something noisy, such as an electric appliance like a refrigerator, which makes strange sounds in the middle of the night?

- Maybe your iguana can see its own image and thinks it's another iguana.

When you start thinking like an iguana, you'll have come a long way to solving the problem and making it a happy, healthy pet. Remember, it may take months before your iguana is comfortable with the stressful environmental changes it endures when it lives in a cage.

PERSONALITY TYPES

Basically, there seem to be two types of iguanas—one that, with proper care and development, becomes one of the most wonderful pets ever known to man; and the high-strung, nervous iguana that may never calm down. Every iguana has its own personality. Given the same basic training, development, environment and patience, some iguanas will be easy to handle and some may never be.

It will take some time and experimentation for you to realize what kind of temperament your iguana has and how you will handle it.

6

Most iguanas have innate dispositions and distinct personalities that change with each stage in the iguana's life.

Iguanas, like people, are who they are.

It is important to remember that iguanas, like people and other pets, can change their behavior over the years. Hopefully, this change is always for the better. Signs of progress with your iguana include easier accessibility, a relaxed disposition and a more comfortable demeanor. But one also should realize that a calm iguana may become less easy to handle or even aggressive over time.

GROWTH STAGES

As your iguana gets older, it will go through different stages of behavioral development. At each stage, different character traits become evident. But the reptile's inherent personality cannot be "improved upon" or "trained."

When you obtain an iguana, you may be obtaining an individual that has a nasty character, or a sweet, mellow disposition or a combination of the two. Or it may have a fearful character, or a dull character, or be a loner, or a mean, nasty critter, or a comedian or a curious and friendly guy. And one iguana can be all of the above! And each of these traits can come out during the different stages of development.

There are marked differences between the behavior of the baby iguana, the teenage iguana and the adult iguana. They, like other animals, go through stages where they will act very differently than they did in their previous stage. Male iguanas in particular may become more aggressive once they reach sexual maturity, especially during the breeding season.

If your iguana suddenly starts acting strange, note the behavior change on your calendar and keep track of it. Think about what could be causing it and what else in the environment changed at that time. If it doesn't improve, talk to an experienced iguana owner or consult a veterinarian.

TEMPERAMENT AND SEX

Male and female iguanas have very different temperaments. It is generalized that males can be more aggressive and independent, and less overtly curious. Generally, the female seems less likely to be interested in investigating the house and would rather be trying to find a hiding spot. Male iguanas become more active and more aggressive when they become mature and attempt to establish a territory. Your adult male will spend much time perched in a prominent place rapidly nodding his head up and down, a behavior known as "head-bobbing." This is iguana talk for "this territory is mine!"

DISPELLING MYTHS

Probably because keeping iguanas as pets is relatively new, there are a lot of myths about how to raise and care for them. This book will dispel a lot of them, and as you get into the feeding and habitat chapters you'll learn how to do things right for your iguana. Because you will inevitably hear a lot of different advice, we're providing this list for your reference. We hope it keeps you from worrying unnecessarily, and keeps your iguana safe from harm.

- Iguanas with orange skin are not necessarily sick. Sometimes their

Be calm and patient with your pet and you will enjoy each other's company for years to come.

skin will appear orange, but it may be no cause for concern. In adult male iguanas, orange skin is a sign that the iguana is ready to breed. However, if the skin turns orange/yellow over a very short amount of time and the iguana is also showing signs of sickness (lethargy, not eating), consult a veterinarian immediately.

- Iguanas are not very intelligent animals. Although they can learn to recognize their keeper and are capable of understanding simple routines, they are not as smart as a dog or a cat.

- A small area to live in will not produce a smaller animal, only an uncomfortable animal. If you keep an iguana in a small cage it will only get more cramped as it gets older.

- Make sure your pet gets real sunlight (not filtered through a window) whenever possible, and use the correct spectrum of ultraviolet lighting to give your pet the best possible substitute when you can't give it sunlight. Artificial lighting is not an alternative to sunlight; it is a substitute.

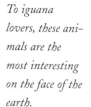

To iguana lovers, these animals are the most interesting on the face of the earth.

- Feeding your iguana dog food will not make it more aggressive. But because, in the wild, iguanas eat no animal protein, iguanas should not be fed any food that has animal protein as part of its ingredients. Iguanas should not be fed crickets, monkey biscuits or dog/cat food. They cannot digest animal fat very well, and eating meat produces deposits on the internal organs, which is very harmful. Some experts think that kidney disease in iguanas may be due to feeding them animal protein in their early years as they are growing. Kidney disease is becoming a more and more common problem in iguanas, which is truly sad. Iguanas cannot be trusted to eat what is good for them. They will eat anything they can find or that is given to them.

- Some experts will tell you that handling or petting an iguana for fifteen minutes a day guarantees it will be tame. Other experts will say that you have to handle the iguana every day for it to get to know or like you. Don't believe them. Every iguana is an individual and doesn't always read the rule book!

THE OTHER PETS— THERE'S A DIFFERENCE

As stated previously, iguanas are not like other pets, especially mammals. They are different from dogs and cats and birds in many respects. Most importantly, puppies and kittens do not consider you to be a threat.

Right from the start, your pet iguana is not sure what to make of you. It may actually be thinking "I don't know what that thing is, but I sure hope it doesn't try to eat me." Your dog or cat never thinks like that. That is why your iguana does not come running to meet you at the door.

The iguana lives its life in fear until otherwise convinced that you mean no harm. So it's important to provide your iguana with safe quarters and a place to be alone while you gain its trust. Handling comes much later. When your iguana is scared or afraid, do not try to handle or pet it. This only increases its fear.

Don't expect too much too soon from a new iguana. Initially, the important signs of progress are a lack of fear when you enter the

9

room and a willingness to be handled. A young iguana may be prone to fits of panic, tail-whipping, biting or running. Hopefully, the young iguana will outgrow these temper tantrums, especially once it becomes more comfortable with its environment. If you think your iguana is progressing too slowly, one thing you might consider is rearranging the environment. You can change the position of the aquarium, the light, the objects inside the enclosure or even the traffic patterns through the room. Sometimes simple changes like these make a world of difference. Remember, iguana owners need to have lots of patience, especially with young iguanas.

CHAPTER TWO

The Illustrious Iguana

The very first thing to realize is that the iguana we are the most familiar with as a pet and the one to which this book is dedicated is the green iguana. Most of the time in this book, when we refer to iguana, we mean the green iguana of pet fame. When we use the term iguana to mean the grouping of lizards called iguana, we'll point that out.

BODY TYPE

Iguana lizards range in habitats from arboreal (tree-dwelling) to semiarboreal. Most iguanas have tails that grow from two to three times their actual body length. These long tails are used as balancing poles when the iguana runs along a tree branch.

The iguana is "cold-blooded" (technically it is an ectotherm), meaning its system cannot generate sufficient body heat to sustain itself. It is dependent on outside heat sources to raise its body temperature, which is why it's critical to have the correct environment for an iguana.

Iguanas hatch from eggs (a single clutch may contain as many as sixty eggs). The female lays the eggs deep in a hole that it digs in the ground. The average length of a newborn iguana is about 7 inches long. If well-fed, an iguana can grow as much as 1½ inches per month. Within a year, it potentially can grow to be about a foot-and-a-half in length. Within three years, it will reach its adult length of 6 feet. Listed below are some distinguishing body features of the green iguana.

FEMORAL PORES—On the underside of each back leg, iguanas have a single row of small, circular holes called femoral pores. Usually, the femoral pores of males are significantly larger and more pronounced than those of females. These pores

The iguana is a cold-blooded reptile, which means it relies on sources of heat from outside its body, like the sun, to raise its body temperature.

produce a waxy substance that helps the male iguana mark his territory. In most green iguanas, the size of these pores can be used to distinguish males from females.

SUBTYMPANIC SCALES—Below the eardrum (tympanum) of all green iguanas there are one to three greatly enlarged scales. These serve as visual signals when the iguana does its head-bobbing territorial display.

PARIETAL EYE—Iguanas have a parietal eye. It is located between the eyes, but a little further toward the back of the head. It does not look so much like a third eye as it does a large gray scale. The parietal eye is sensitive to light cycles, probably aiding in the breeding cycles.

TONGUE—Iguanas have a short, thick tongue and will attempt to taste or lick a great many things—including their owners! It is normal for the very tip of the tongue to appear to be more red in color than the rest of the tongue.

TEETH—The iguana's teeth are round at the root and have ridges on them like a serrated edge. The teeth

This iguana has raised its retractable crest.

are described as pleurodont, which means that they actually protrude from the side of the jawbone rather than grow from sockets above the jawbone like human teeth.

CREST—Both males and females have a row of large pointy scales located down the length of the spine and tail. These scales stand up and retract, and tend to be larger on males than females. When trying to impress females and when fighting with other animals over territory, males will do everything they can to make the crest more pronounced, thus appearing bigger to their opponents.

DEWLAP—The iguana has a large, hanging fold of skin under its throat called a dewlap. This is expanded and displayed in courtship or in battle. Again, in males they tend to be larger than in females. During mating, females also display their dewlaps.

COLOR AND SIZE

Individual green iguanas exhibit a variety of shades and colors, depending on what part of Central or South America the iguana originally came from. For example, iguanas from Brazil tend to be more blue, whereas those from El

Iguanas aren't always green. Just take a look at this beautiful spiny-tailed iguana from Panama.

Salvador are a more vivid green and Mexican iguanas may even be orange. Striped coloring has been noted on iguanas from Guatemala and other Central American countries. Some farms have begun breeding albino stock. These are more yellowish-green than white, but they do have a fair amount of pink in their skin and scales. Regardless of their original color and pattern, as iguanas age, the colors fade and become more subtle.

ENVIRONMENT

Typically, we think of the green iguana's natural habitat as a tropical environment of lush vegetation and fresh water. But some green iguanas live in more desert-like surroundings and some live near saltwater. Green iguanas are found in areas where temperatures reach 80° to 100°F (or even higher) during the day and drop to 70°F at night.

A day spent with an iguana in Costa Rica, for example, would include feasting on the surrounding vegetation, climbing up trees and vines, basking in a sunny spot, retreating to the shade, feasting on more vegetation, more basking and shading, making its way to a pool or stream for a drink and possibly a swim, a few more nibbles and then a night of sleep. Iguanas are climbers, swimmers, leaf eaters and sun-bathers.

How the Iguana Got Its Name

"Iguana" is the interpretation Spanish explorers gave to the name the native American Caribbean Indians called these lizards, which was *iwana.* One of the earliest known fossil lizards was named Paliguana by paleontologists, which means "ancient iguana." The very first dinosaur to be discovered was named Iguanodon, which means "iguana tooth" because its teeth resembled those of a very large iguana. Dinosaurs are not actually closely related to lizards.

All iguanas are included in the family *Iguanidae,* which contains eight genera, or kinds, of iguanas. These genera include *Amblyrhynchus, Brachylophus, Conolophus, Ctenosaura, Cyclura, Dipsosaurus, Iguana* and *Sauromalus.*

Each of the eight genera includes many species of iguana. Listed below are the more popular varieties of iguana—the ones you can find at your pet store, breeder or zoo.

Green Iguana (*Iguana iguana*)—This is the most commonly kept house pet in the Iguanid family. Although it is most correct to call this animal the green iguana, many people just call it iguana, incorrectly thinking that this is the only lizard called an iguana.

Wild green iguanas are suffering from habitat loss as rainforest is destroyed, and are legally protected in most of their native countries. They are also protected by the Convention on International Trade in Endangered Species (CITES). Nearly all of the iguanas available in the United States have been

15

Iguanas have recently been introduced to some parts of the United States, such as south Florida, where the climate is tropical.

captive-bred on commercial "iguana farms." This iguana is native to Central and South America, ranging all the way from northern Mexico to parts of Paraguay. Iguanas have also been found on islands in the Lesser Antilles. Recently, iguanas have been introduced to some parts of the United States, most notably to areas with similar environments (tropical climates with lots of moisture and foliage), such as south Florida.

Of all the iguanas, green iguanas are the most arboreal and were at one time known as "tree iguanas." They are vegetarian reptiles

Iguanas require warmth, sunlight and humidity for good health.

throughout their entire life. Iguanas have been known to eat more than fifty different types of plants, but they prefer to eat the leaves of the types of vegetation found in their environment. As is true of many other reptiles, the iguana is a strong swimmer. Some have been recorded spending a half hour underwater before coming up for air.

A healthy green iguana, given the room to roam and grow, may get to be 6 to 7 feet in length (two-thirds of which is tail) and weigh up to twenty-five to thirty pounds. If you allow them to, they will dominate your house. The most important thing to remember with an iguana in regards to its needs is that it is a tropical to semitropical animal, which means it requires warmth, sunlight and humidity for good health. It is diurnal, which means it is active during the daylight hours.

CHUCKWALLA (*SAUROMALUS OBESUS*)—The chuckwalla is very easy to identify as it looks like a black or brown colored fatter version of the *Iguana iguana*. A native of the southwestern American deserts, the chuckwalla uses its girth to its advantage in the wild. When

This desert iguana is at home in the cactus.

confronted by an aggressor, the chuckwalla slithers into the narrowest of cracks and then puffs itself up, lodging itself into the rocks so that it cannot be pulled out.

DESERT IGUANA (*DIPSOSAURUS DORSALIS*)—

This species is generally smaller than the popular *Iguana iguana*. Found mostly in the southwestern United States and Mexico, it is a desert dweller. There are many state laws that prohibit the capture of wild desert iguanas, and most of the ones that come up for sale to the common hobbyist are bred in captivity by experts.

RHINOCEROS AND ROCK IGUANAS (*CYCLURA* SPP.)—

These iguanas are much larger than the common green iguana. There are many varieties of this particular lizard, and it is the largest subset of the iguana family. Although they are extremely handsome lizards, they are also extremely expensive, when available.

SPINY-TAILED OR BLACK IGUANA (*CTENOSAURA* SPP.)—

This iguana ranges from Mexico to Panama and is even found on some Colombian islands. The *Ctenosaura* genera lists nine species. They are quite commonly available and some

This Fiji iguana from the Fiji Islands is an endangered species.

of the rarer species are being bred on farms in several countries. Some are quite affordable.

For the most part, this group tends to be dull-colored, especially as they mature into adults. Even so, there are a few species that are quite visually captivating.

Ctenosaura species are differentiated from other iguanas by their spiny tail. The tail is usually not as long as it is on other iguanas, but is easily distinguished by the winding, sharp, raised scales that protrude from it. Mature adults use this tail as a rather intimidating weapon.

Almost all of the species listed here grow no longer than 3 feet in length, and, as with most lizards, the females tend to be slightly smaller. Many of these animals are imported, but captive breeding, especially in the United States, is making these species more and more available.

IGUANAS IN AMERICA

For years, iguanas have been popular pets, but few attempts were made to differentiate among the various species. They were always sold under the name iguana, regardless if the type was a chuckwalla, a green iguana or a rhinoceros iguana. In the

1950s, iguanas were still being sold under the incorrect name of "Chinese Dragons." In fact, several dinosaur science fiction movies of the 1940s and 1950s actually starred iguanas that were enlarged by trick photography.

It was not until the 1960s and 1970s that iguanas first drew serious interest, and zoologists and experts began to try to separate out the various genera.

WHERE IGUANAS COME FROM TODAY

Breeding farms have both increased the population of iguanas as well as brought down the price of iguanas. Breeding these reptiles in captivity has also helped people learn more about them, specifically their husbandry needs and their unique, interesting behavior.

There are many advantages to the pet owner of owning farm-bred rather than wild-caught animals.

The first and greatest advantage is to the animals themselves. Captured iguanas, born in the wild, usually adapt inadequately to life with people and make poor pets. Iguanas are timid creatures and tend not to adjust very well to significant changes. When they are forced to live with people, these changes include living in artificial environments and being handled often. They are not used to handlers, and this creates a lot of stress, which may lead the iguana to bite. While some of the bites are not serious, iguanas have teeth and they can draw blood. But the message is clear: Let go and leave me alone! This does not make for a good human-animal relationship. Even more important, these new stresses lead to poor health of the iguana and then, sometimes, to its demise. Because of these stresses, a great many wild-caught iguanas stop eating, get sick and die in captivity.

CHAPTER THREE

Choosing Your Iguana

A pet shop is the most common place for beginners to go to obtain an iguana. However, before you walk into the pet store, it is important to know what questions you should ask the salespeople and how to work with them on finding the right iguana for you.

WHAT TO LOOK FOR

Physical Traits

A healthy iguana is active and has a full, thick tail base. When iguanas are sick and lose weight, the tail base becomes thin and the bones almost protrude through the skin. The best age to purchase pet iguanas is when they are 3 to 5 months old because they are strong enough to withstand change but young enough to adjust to changes in their environment.

Baby iguanas are about a foot long from nose to tail. You want a new healthy iguana to be sleek, bright green and alert.

Babies are inquisitive and are not afraid of being handled, though it's important not to overhandle them when you bring one home. In a healthy baby iguana, the body must be taut and sinewy. They are active, not lethargic.

If the baby looks bloated, whether in the limbs or in the stomach, then avoid it; this is usually a sign that there is something seriously wrong. If there are any swellings along the jaw, avoid that iguana as well. There should be no discharge around the nose or mouth, and there should be no evidence of burns on the skin.

Older vs. Younger Pets

In general, babies are usually more active and more tame than adults. When you're inspecting baby iguanas from the pet shop, make sure there are no quick movements or loud voices, and avoid rough handling.

You may see adults in the pet shop. Literally and figuratively, approach these older iguanas with

Your baby iguana should be sleek, bright green and alert.

WHAT TO LOOK FOR IN AN IGUANA

Age and Size

You want a young iguana, 3 to 5 months old, between a foot and a foot and a half long. These are usually less afraid, more curious and have an easier time adjusting to domesticated life. It will be easier in the long run to tame these younger animals. Beginners should stick to younger iguanas, and not try to take on troublesome animals.

Skin

You want a bright green color, not unlike the new shoots of a plant. Don't buy an iguana that looks waxy, pale or yellowish—signs of sure death.

Body

You want an iguana who shows no signs of physical damage, and who has a thick tail base and a lean, sinewy body. You should not buy an iguana with wounds of any kind.

Behavior

You want an alert iguana who doesn't run when you approach the aquarium. It should show some interest in you and should have smooth movements. It should not be frozen with its eyes shut or running around trying to find an escape hatch.

Appetite

You want an iguana who's hungry when the food dish is set down or who will take food from your hand. Don't buy an iguana who's not interested in food.

caution. Some of them may be previously owned pets that are now in the pet store because of unacceptable behavior traits. Ask the salesperson about the animal's health and behavior, and ask why an adult is for sale.

Character Traits

Whether a baby or an adult, the first thing you should analyze is the fear quotient. Is the baby or the adult frozen with fear when a person approaches? If so, don't buy it. You should be allowed to hold the iguana at the pet shop. If it doesn't move, doesn't lick you and has its eyes closed, then this is not your iguana.

You want an iguana that keeps moving in a steady, not neurotic, fashion. If an iguana stretches in front of you the first time that it sees you, that's a comfortable, well-adjusted, confident iguana. Take that one!

You should also slowly, gently stroke the iguana along the length of its back to see how it reacts to human contact. Any sudden movements by the iguana may be an indication of its willingness to run and its discomfort with people. If the clerk will let you, you may also want to see if the iguana will stay on your forearm. If it does, then this is also a good sign that it is used to people.

The Skin

One of the most important things to look for when choosing a healthy iguana is the skin color and texture. Baby iguanas should normally have bright green skin, no matter what part of the world they are from. Very rarely they can be blue-green, which is normal for that color variation. However, most importantly, you are looking for color vibrancy.

The colors, no matter what shade, should be intense. Any dull, pasty or pale-looking iguanas should be quickly discarded from consideration. Also, any iguana that has a yellowish-green hue should not be purchased, as this coloration may indicate impending illness.

As iguanas grow in size and age, they lose their intense color and become a grayish green. Some will change to a reddish-orange color, which is very much in demand. But whether you're looking at a baby or an older iguana, you'll be able to tell if the skin is healthy by the overall tone of the colors and the elasticity and texture of the skin.

23

Testing an iguana's comfort level is easy: Just place the iguana on your hand or forearm and see if it stays. If it does, then the iguana is comfortable and likes people.

The skin should not hang from the iguana's sides or belly. There should be no scars or open wounds on the iguana. If there are dark areas on the skin, these may be indications of previous injuries, such as those sustained from burns or fights.

If the iguana is shedding, that is not a problem. That indicates it is growing, which means it is eating, implying that it is at least a little more comfortable with its surroundings than other iguanas its age. If it is shedding, make certain the skin underneath looks healthy.

Eyes

An iguana's eyes should not be wide open; their eyes should be relaxed and clear. Wide-open eyes indicate fear or apprehension. The eyes should also not be closed. This may mean eye disease or even that the iguana is ill and too sick to open its eyes. Look for any scars on the surface of the eye.

Licking

If the iguana you have your eye on sticks its tongue out and starts licking you, it shows that you have a

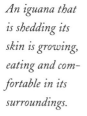

An iguana that is shedding its skin is growing, eating and comfortable in its surroundings.

confident, secure animal in front of you. If it doesn't lick you voluntarily, put your finger near its mouth and see if it will lick you. If it does, that's also a good sign. Does it lick when it walks? That's a good sign, too. An iguana will not lick when it is scared or intimidated.

Sometimes a baby iguana will lick your finger and then bite it. It's just confusing your finger with food. This also says that it has a healthy appetite.

THE FINGER TEST

This is a simple character test you can conduct on a store iguana. While you're handling an iguana, hold your finger to its mouth. A lick is a sign of submission; a good thing for a pet iguana. A bite might indicate a more aggressive animal, but that's no reason to reject it; this animal may just be hungry. If the iguana is frozen in place, it is probably very afraid.

CHAPTER FOUR

Homecoming

ability to range over a large territory. They are relatively active and walk, swim and climb. Obviously, you can't offer up the house to your iguana, but there are ways to compromise to keep both your iguana and you happy.

HOUSING REQUIREMENTS

Space

One of the basic requirements that you need to consider is space. An iguana needs space to roam and a space to hide. A safe enclosure must be provided so that the iguana cannot escape and so nothing can get

How you house your iguana is the key to how well you maintain its health.

It is important to remember that, in the wild, iguanas have the

into your iguana's cage. It is heart-breaking when an iguana crawls out of its enclosure and gets either lost or injured.

Also, it is of the utmost impor-tance that nothing be allowed to threaten your iguana, especially other house pets. The common house cat, for example, is largely responsible for the dwindling iguana populations in the Caribbean. The iguana's living space should also be a safe distance from loud noises or away from the household traffic.

Temperature

Another important, basic considera-tion is temperature. Because the iguana is a cold-blooded animal, it depends on the ambient temperature to regulate its internal temperature. An iguana must have an area inside its enclosure that reaches tempera-tures of 85° to 100°F, especially dur-ing the day. The temperature should not fall below 70°F.

If your iguana spends all of its time under the heat lamp (especially if its skin is taking on a darker-than-normal color), it means that it is cold. Raise the temperature in the cage. Conversely, if your iguana huddles in a far corner away from the heat lamp, it is too hot.

But you don't want to bake your iguana, either. Be sure there's a place in the enclosure where the iguana

A heat lamp is placed on the left side of this half-grown iguana's cage in order to keep the other side of the cage cool.

can go to get out of the heat, whether it's a corner away from a heat source or a ledge to hide under. Place a thermometer in the basking area to be certain that the heated area is not getting too hot for your iguana.

Heat lamps are a potential burn hazard for your iguana. Never place a heat lamp inside the cage where the iguana can touch it. Put it outside over one portion of the screen lid.

Environment

Just like you, the iguana is comfortable when it is comfortable with its surroundings. Iguanas are more happy when their enclosures include things like tree limbs, places to hide, an elevated shelf or two and maybe even a giant bowl of water. A cardboard or wooden box placed in the enclosure will satisfy an iguana's need to hide when it is scared and provide a place to sleep comfortably at night.

The very best place to situate your iguana's enclosure is by a window where it might get exposure to sunlight. But remember, the ultraviolet (UV) light spectrum so needed by iguanas for their health does not go through the glass in the windows. Being by a window is not a substitute for direct exposure to sunlight or artificial ultraviolet light.

An elevated perching area will give your iguana the sense of natural safety that, as a tree-climber, it craves.

An elevated perching area will also make an iguana feel better. It gives it the sense of natural safety that all tree-climbing animals crave.

Food and Water

Just like all living things, iguanas require water and the correct diet to live a long life. An important rule to remember is not to feed it what it wants; feed it what it needs. A very basic diet recommendation includes a variety of vegetables and plant materials and a very small amount of fruits.

A bowl of water is mandatory. Depending on the size of the bowl, your iguana may want to bathe in it. That's fine; just remember to wash it and fill it back up with cool, clean water. In fact, you may want to provide a water bowl for drinking and a larger water bowl for swimming.

WHAT KIND OF ENCLOSURE?

Most people prefer to initially house their baby iguana in an aquarium. As the iguana grows, people will change to larger enclosures. Although birdcages are usually bigger and offer more space to roam,

baby iguanas are small enough to slip through the bars. Observe your baby closely and see what it can or cannot do. That will determine the size of the initial enclosure you will need for your new pet. Because young iguanas grow quickly, you will be constantly upgrading the size of your cage, unless you initially obtain one large enough for a full-grown adult.

Regardless of which kind of enclosure you choose, never allow your baby iguana to roam around the house unsupervised. There are too many places in your house in which it could be injured or lost. Crawl spaces and heating vents are your biggest enemies.

Aquariums vs. Cages

There are good and bad aspects about aquariums. They can be heavy and difficult to move. Another problem is due to the glass, which blocks the beneficial rays of the sun and also intensifies the heat. Sometimes this can cause a burn on your iguana's skin or, if it gets hot enough, your iguana can die from heat exposure.

Aquariums, being enclosed on five of six sides, can potentially lead

Most baby iguanas are small enough to be housed in a thirty-gallon tank, but when the iguana starts to grow, both you and the iguana will prefer another type of enclosure. When an iguana grows beyond 30 inches (including the length of the tail), you really need to build a large cage or pen.

A cage offers the best possible air circulation and does not interfere with the light from the sun. If the cage is tall enough, you can add shelves or branches for the iguana to climb on. Cages are also less likely to break and are lighter to carry.

It is important to note that an iguana's claws can easily become entangled in ordinary window screen, leading to broken toes. In any homemade cage, it is best to use hardware cloth with a $1/4$-inch mesh instead of window screen. The hardware cloth is also more durable and less likely to be torn by the iguana (iguanas can escape by clawing their way through a window screen).

It is important that iguanas have enough space to feel comfortable. A 6-foot animal obviously needs something much larger than a 6-inch cage. For adult iguanas in warmer areas of the country, many enthusiasts have outdoor enclosures for the

Cages, like the one pictured here, offer the best possible air circulation and do not interfere with the light from the sun.

to unsanitary conditions. They may be difficult to clean, especially if moisture accumulates in the substrate. Also, if there are unsanitary conditions, the odor level will greatly increase, making for some unpleasant living conditions for both your iguana and your nose. Actually, this is a serious condition, as odors that increase in this closed environment may be toxic to your iguana's respiratory system, predisposing it to respiratory diseases.

day and smaller inside ones for sleeping at night.

A 4-foot-long iguana would require a cage with dimensions of 6 feet (height) by 6 feet (width) by 30 inches (depth). Cages or pens can be easily built and casters are put on the cages so that they are easily moved.

An advantage to cages is that because they are easier to move than glass enclosures, you can take them out on a nice day and put them in the yard so that your iguana can get some natural sunlight. That bountiful natural sunlight will be a big treat. *A special note to remember, though:* Do not leave the cage unattended as you never know what neighborhood pets or wild animals are around to harass your little green friend. Always make sure you are there for the iguana. Also, make sure your iguana always has a shaded area to retreat to when it becomes too warm.

EQUIPPING THE CAGE

Iguanas look for height and they need sun. Iguanas also like to cool

Equipping your iguana's cage with foliage is a great way to provide shade for your pet—and it isn't bad for holding dinner either.

off in shady areas—they need plants, and they need water. Their craving for climbing can be solved by placing a tree limb, branch or even a shelf somewhere in the enclosure. Iguanas naturally want to climb, and once they've ascended, they like to rest there and soak up sunlight. The limb you put in the iguana's cage should always be one-and-a-half to two times larger than your iguana.

Foliage is important because it provides shade when the animal wants to cool down. It also provides a hiding space to camouflage the iguana if intimidated by sudden movements or a guest. Unfortunately, iguanas will eat all plants you put in with them, so it is better to decorate your iguana's domain with plastic plants.

Artificial Flowers

There is no shame in using plastic plants in your iguana's cage. They will inevitably be sampled, but not eaten. They can be washed and reused if they get soiled, and they provide your pet with shade and camouflage comfort. Plastic plants help you avoid the problems of toxic plants and also do not interfere with your iguana's diet.

If you don't want your iguana to eat the plants in its cage, try decorating its domain with plastic or silk plants and flowers; they will be sampled, but not eaten.

SHOULD YOU LET YOUR IGUANA OUT?

Why You Shouldn't

As your iguana gets older, tamer and more accustomed to you, you may be tempted to allow it to roam around the house. There are many reasons not to give in to this temptation. When iguanas roam the house, they can get hurt, as few

You should iguana-proof your home before allowing your iguana to roam around—it might not be prepared for the things it finds.

people iguana-proof their house. To this extent, you need to directly supervise your pet while it is free in the house.

Other than the threat to your iguana's safety, there is another good reason to keep the iguana in its cage. Few homes are warm enough for your iguana's metabolism. Most homes are kept with temperatures in the 70s, and this is too low for an iguana's metabolism and good health. And, if your iguana is meandering around the house, it will not be under the ultraviolet light source you have so nicely set up in its cage. Therefore, your pet will miss out on a vital aspect of its environment.

If you could provide an area where the iguana was able to maintain the high body temperature and be exposed to direct sunlight or ultraviolet light, it would be less dangerous for it to be out of its cage.

If You Do

Many iguanas only want to sit on top of their cages to get closer to the light. Others want to investigate. If you think your iguana is ready to join you and your family in the rest of the house, first find an area that can be closed off and that's completely safe to roam around in, like a spare bedroom or the kitchen. Make sure all sharp objects and anything the iguana can swallow are cleared away.

Anytime you let an iguana wander, you must keep in mind that they can and will climb almost anything, including drapery, any kinds of cords hanging down, furniture, bookcases and so forth. This is not something you want to do with especially young iguanas. A 4-foot iguana is hard to lose in your living room; a 6-inch lizard is easy to lose in a house.

SUBSTRATE

Newspaper

Whether you are using a cage or an aquarium, the bottom of the enclosure needs to be lined with something. The most popular and safest lining material is newspaper. Some people place ripped-up or shredded newspaper on the bottom, while others prefer to line the enclosure as they would a birdcage, with flat sheets. Either way, newspaper is the easiest, safest and cheapest way to line the bottom. Another advantage to using newspaper is that it is easy to know when it is soiled and ready to be changed so that your iguana does not walk around in a messy cage.

Pellets

Two other preferred substrates are rabbit pellets and alfalfa pellets. Even if your iguana decides to eat this, that's okay; it's edible and even provides nutrients that it needs. They are very absorbent, which keeps the cage looking clean but may fool you into not realizing how dirty the substrate really is. The disadvantage to pellets is that they get moldy when wet and must be cleaned and replaced often.

Astroturf

Some people recommend carpeting or Astroturf. Carpeting is not a good idea. It is easily soiled and hard to clean, and the iguana may even try to eat it. Astroturf, on the other hand, works well in most cages, but is not very absorbent and must be cleaned often.

Many experts use Astroturf and put a small sandbox in the corner. Do not use cat litter, as your iguana will eat it and block its intestines! It is also important to note that iguanas sometimes defecate in their water bowl. It is important to change the water every day for this reason.

Other Types

You may see recommendations for such things as cedar chips, orchid bark or pine shavings. This may give the cage a more natural look than newspaper, but there can be problems if these types of materials are used. Fecal material and food can be buried in the shavings, allowing bacteria and fungi to grow unchecked. Because iguanas are highly susceptible to all kinds of infections and diseases, this buildup of microorganisms is not good for the health of your iguana. Also, the aroma of these shavings, especially cedar chips, may even be toxic to iguanas and other lizards.

Another reason to avoid wood-chip substrates is that iguanas will eat these shavings. If your iguana ate this material, it could get an intestinal infection, or worse, a blocked intestine that would necessitate surgery. For these simple reasons, many experts avoid wood shavings altogether.

Although realistic looking, it is not recommended to use dirt or sand as a substrate. Your iguana can ingest this material, causing an infection or, worse, a blockage in the intestines. This is very serious and can lead to the death of your iguana. Also, sand and dirt are not very hygienic. Bacteria and fungal organisms are harbored in this material and can cause disease and death in your iguana.

REGULATING THE HEAT

Iguanas come from areas where temperatures reach the high 80s and 90s and even higher. If you are lucky enough to live in an area where your iguana is naturally exposed to these kinds of temperatures, all you need to do is make sure your iguana is getting enough light. However, iguana owners in the rest of the world must re-create temperature conditions to ensure the health of

35

Baby iguanas enjoy spending much of their time under the basking lights.

*Both incandes-
cent light and
florescent light
are commercially
available for
iguanas and
other lizards.*

36

your pet. Over the years, people have tried various methods to bring heat and light into their iguana's man-made environment.

There are basically two ways you can give your iguana heat: (1) with lights (incandescent, reflector and full-spectrum bulbs) and (2) with ceramic heating elements. These are mushroom-shaped devices that screw into an ordinary light socket. They provide radiant heat but do not give off any light. The electric "hot rocks" or "sizzle stones" that are found in pet shops should never be used for an iguana. They can produce severe burns.

HOW MUCH LIGHT?

Because iguanas are diurnal, the light should be left on all day but turned off at night. Baby iguanas are especially fond of the lights and their basking times, and will spend as much time under the lights as possible. For the first few days, you should leave the light on as long as possible and see how your pet reacts. You can then best judge what hours of the day are important for your animal to bask. In general, iguanas will prefer a twelve-hour-on and twelve-hour-off cycle, which mimics the length of the tropical day.

The iguana's system needs sunlight to synthesize vitamin D_3 to help build its bones. Iguanas use the ultraviolet wavelengths in sunlight to manufacture vitamin D_3 in their skin. Vitamin D_3 is necessary for the proper extraction of calcium from its food. If the iguana does not have access to UV light, or if the phosphorus/calcium ration in its food is improper, its body cannot use the calcium in its food, and tries to compensate by extracting calcium from its own bones. This produces a lethal disease called metabolic bone disease, or MBD. It is the pet owner's responsibility to make sure the iguana is getting as much real, direct sunlight as possible or, in its place, artificial UV light. Be sure to use a fluorescent UV light that was specifically designed for reptiles; the artificial "full spectrum sunlamps" used for plants do not provide the proper wavelengths for iguanas.

HOW MUCH SUN?

Exposing your iguana to real sunlight is not as difficult as it sounds, especially if you live in a warm area of the world. If you take it into the sun for about an hour or so a day, you should be able to maintain a happy, healthy iguana. It is important that baby iguanas get as much real sunlight as possible.

Of course, the best thing to do is place your iguana's enclosure near an open window where direct sunlight can reach the animal. It is important in these instances to make sure that the lid to the cage is securely fastened to prevent escape. It is also important that the iguana have a shaded area to cool off in when it wants to.

CHAPTER FIVE

Handling Your Iguana

It's important to remember that if you saw an iguana in the wild, it would run away, slither off into the water or do anything else it could to get away from you. It wouldn't come near you for all the juicy green leaves in the world. Iguanas are solitary creatures and they don't even like hanging around with each other, except during mating season.

IN THE BEGINNING

The first tricks to master are quietness and slow, deliberate movements. You need to build trust. Sudden or fast movements are those of a predator. Someone who moves slowly is probably not interested in eating the iguana, and at least the animal can watch you better, and hopefully feel more comfortable.

After it is apparent that the iguana is comfortable, then you can begin interaction.

How do you know when the iguana is comfortable with you? When it stops fleeing when you come in the room, it is comfortable with you. When it stops freezing in place when you are near, it is comfortable with you.

When you come to feed it, does it hide, or does it come eagerly toward the food? With an iguana, if it doesn't flee or freeze while you are in its presence, then you are making progress. This painstakingly slow process may take up to two to three weeks or longer. It depends completely on the personality of the iguana, each of which is an individual.

FIRST TOUCH

When you're ready to attempt to touch the iguana for the first time, remember again that your actions should be slow, deliberate and quiet. A good way to acclimate the iguana to touch is to feed it by hand. This builds trust between you and the animal. When you're going to pick up your iguana, make sure you offer it your hand. Once it knows you, it will, given the proper personality, learn to walk onto your hand.

Iguanas hate being grabbed and picked up roughly. It is the best and fastest way to destroy the trust you have built up with the animal. Never attempt to catch your pet by the head. Instead, pet him on the back

With an iguana, if it doesn't flee or freeze while you are in its presence, then you are making progress.

of the head and on the sides. These first attempts at handling should last no more than ten to fifteen minutes in the beginning of your relationship. And they should be repeated every day.

Eventually you should be able to hold the younger or baby iguana in your hands and let the iguana run back and forth from hand to hand. It may try to escape, but gentle handling and persistence eventually show the iguana that there is nothing to fear. After several weeks, the iguana should seem calmer during these sessions.

40

When responding to what it thinks is a threat, your iguana may extend its dewlap.

WHEN NOT TO HOLD IT

One thing to remember is never to pick up an iguana, especially a male iguana, when it is in its most aggressive posture. This is when it is standing as high up on its legs as it can, with spines erect, and with its mouth open.

In responding to what it thinks is a threat, the iguana will expand the dewlap under its mouth and open its mouth. Its tail will definitely twitch. Don't even think about handling it, especially if it is an older male. There is the chance, with an older male, that you could get bitten and/or scratched. Iguanas can also lash out with their long tail, causing painful welts.Come back a little later and see if you can start over.

HOLDING YOUR IGUANA

It is important that you don't hold an iguana like you would a puppy or a newborn baby. There are two right ways to hold an iguana and a thousand wrong ones. The most important thing in holding an iguana properly is to support the chest and

Never take your iguana outside without a harness.

the tail area. Many needless injuries are caused by owners who grab their iguanas by the tail (which often breaks off) or by a limb. This is not the way to approach the handling of an iguana. You could easily injure your pet.

Some people will hold the chest from underneath with one hand and the back two legs and tail with the other. The other position is to let the iguana rest along the length of your forearm, carrying the iguana like a football. Either way you are supporting the chest and tail area firmly, without causing undue stress to the animal. If you use your hands to pin the iguana's legs back along the sides of its body, and clamp its tail between your arm and body, even an aggressive iguana can be safely carried without fear of scratching or tail-lashing.

TAKING YOUR IGUANA WITH YOU

Though many experts do not advise novices to take their iguanas outside without putting them in some kind of sun cage or other portable enclosure, there is a time when you can finally take your iguana out for a walk. You have to be sure, though, that your iguana can handle the experience. Being naturally reserved, solitary creatures, this can be too overwhelming for your pet. You have to train it to accept a harness with a lead or to stay on your arm or shoulder with the harness on while you're out.

To make sure it will be fun for both you and your pet, start small. If your iguana accepts having the harness on its body, let it wear it around the house. Give it a favorite snack so

SUNLIGHT AGGRESSION

Many iguanas become hyperactive after spending time in direct sunlight. Your iguana will resist being picked up and may run when you approach. Don't take this personally and don't look at it as a step backward. Merely take the iguana back inside and let it calm down. In a number of hours, it will be fine.

When acclimating your iguana to the outside world, begin on the front lawn and gradually extend your travel time and area.

it associates the harness with something pleasant. If your iguana does not want to wear it, don't force the issue. Put the harness away and try some other time.

As your iguana becomes used to the harness, leave it on for longer periods of time, and start walking alongside the iguana with the harness on it. Again, getting treats for walks on the harness in the house will help make them pleasant experiences for your pet.

The Outside World

Make your first excursion one around the yard, then down the street, gradually extending the area you travel and only if your iguana seems comfortable. When you're out, discourage people from reaching out to touch your iguana unless it is well socialized. Tell them you're getting it used to being outside with you, and that when your iguana is ready, you'll let them touch it.

An important warning to those who take their iguanas outdoors: When your housebound iguana is taken outside and experiences natural sunlight, its mood may rapidly change. Iguanas exposed to the sun can become more energetic and more aggressive. It will be unpleasant for you to have a surly iguana on your shoulder, and it may bite you or someone else. The iguana may even

42

try to run away if it is not properly restrained.

If your iguana cannot handle these types of excursions, don't force it to endure these parading gestures. It may cause irreparable damage to the iguana's confidence and your relationship with your pet. Also, if highly stressed like this, the iguana's health could deteriorate, all for the sake of a walk through town or the mall. Don't do it. For those iguanas who are capable of handling such travel, have fun.

If your iguana is comfortable around you and other people, and you start and build up steadily, the two of you may enjoy many walks together. Regardless of whether your iguana is able to travel or not, the joys of befriending these animals are many.

DON'T KISS YOUR IGUANA

Neither children nor adults should ever let their lips touch the iguana or put their own fingers into its mouth. Also, owners must always wash their hands after handling their iguana. This is because iguanas can carry salmonella, an infectious bacteria.

43

CHAPTER SIX

Positively Nutritious

Variety is the spice of life. It is as true for iguanas as it is for people. Don't expect your iguana to be very happy if it gets the same food night after night. Nor will it be very healthy.

Iguanas will eat what they want and not necessarily what is good for them. It is up to you to monitor their diets closely. They need a balanced diet just like we do. Some iguanas, as they get older, are extremely stubborn and resistant to change. There is the great risk that your iguana would die before changing its eating habits. So it's important to start your iguana on a varied diet as soon you obtain it.

Iguanas are called folivores—leaf-eating animals. Based on the natural habits of iguanas, it is best to feed your iguana only plant material.

FEEDING BABY IGUANAS

Hatchlings and baby iguanas can be fed the same vegetables as adults. But these young iguanas may benefit from having their food chopped and shredded into many small pieces.

Fast-Growing Lizards

The hatchling can survive up to three days on its yolk sack. Within three years, it will increase its total body weight by 100 times.

Because iguanas grow so quickly, they need a sufficient amount of calcium in their diets. Iguanas that lack

GET OUT YOUR FOOD PROCESSOR

All food to be given to the iguana, especially if young, must be cut up or shredded. This will promote healthy eating and your pet will avoid choking. Food processors are an invaluable aid in preparing your iguana's meals.

calcium tend to grow slowly and exhibit metabolic bone disease leading to skeletal problems. It's important to feed the proper ratio of calcium to phosphorous, because phosphorous interferes with the iguana's ability to use calcium from its food. You want high calcium and

45

Make feeding time a little easier for your baby by chopping and shredding its veggies.

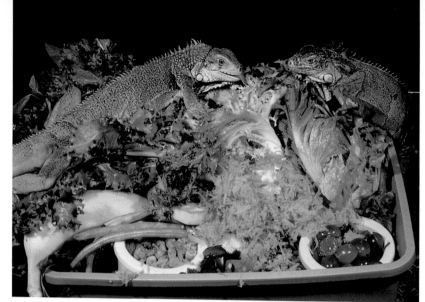

These iguanas enjoy a big salad that has been sprinkled with a powdered vitamin supplement.

low phosphorous in all the food you offer your pet (the ideal ratio is 2:1).

COMMERCIAL PRODUCTS

There is an ever-increasing number of new iguana pet care products out on the market, especially where food is concerned. If the food is made from anything other than vegetable material, you should not feed it to your iguana. Check out the types of vegetables listed in the ingredients. If there is a lot of cornmeal and other starchy vegetables, this is probably not the best food for your iguana. If you don't have the time or inclination to feed a 100 percent natural diet, make sure that no more than 15 percent of the overall diet is a commercial mixture.

Vitamins & Minerals

There are a number of vitamin supplements available on the market. Until enough research is performed in regard to iguana nutrition, we will never know the exact requirements for this group of animals. Therefore, it is a good idea to use a commercial vitamin supplement.

Some people suggest making up a large salad for your iguana and then taking a vitamin tablet or vitamin powder and crushing it into small pieces, spreading it throughout the salad. Most pet iguanas will also need extra calcium added to their diet.

One word of caution: Use a calcium supplement that does not contain any other ingredients, especially no phosphorus and no vitamin D_3. Phosphorous can bind calcium and should not be in a mineral additive, There is mounting evidence that vitamin D_3 given by mouth is not effective and possibly may harm iguanas, so don't give a calcium supplement that has it. Calcium supplement should be added to every other meal. Be careful not to overdo it—too much calcium in the diet is just as harmful to the iguana as too little. Just a pinch is sufficient.

FEEDING SCHEDULES

Babies

Baby iguanas need to be fed every day, twice a day. For hatchlings, a plate of baby food or pureed food should be left out on a flat dish. Make sure they get various vegetables and few fruits. Be sure to alternate food types. It is extremely important to widen the palate of the iguana at an early age, and make sure you don't spoil it by feeding it the same food each day. After awhile, it will eat nothing else. You

ABOUT ICEBERG LETTUCE

Iguanas love lettuce. However, it must be noted that the most commonly available type of lettuce, known as "iceberg," is not particularly good for your iguana. Iceberg lettuce consists largely of cellulose and water and carries few nutrients. It can be called the junk food of the iguana world. Some types of lettuce have no redeeming nutritional value for the iguana. They're like potato chips, nachos or cheese curls. In small doses, they're fine, but don't make them a large part of your pet's diet. If your iguana is already addicted, then work hard to change the diet. Other types of lettuce, like romaine or redleaf, are more nutritious. In the long run, you'll have a much happier, healthier pet!

have to expand these animals' taste buds while they're young.

Adults

A healthy adult iguana needs to be fed only every other day.

WATER

Make sure there is always fresh water somewhere in a bowl inside the enclosure. Change the water once a day.

THE SUN IS FOOD

One way to look at the sun is that it injects nutrients into the iguana's skin—naturally! The effect of the sun is to increase the body's level of calcium. Exposure to sun rays is the "magic trick," the best thing you can do for your iguana. Unfortunately, some people still set the iguana by the glass window "in sunlight," failing to understand that the glass is blocking the ultraviolet rays.

DIETARY GUIDELINES

The following is a guide by which you should feed your iguana. It lists different groups of nutrients and states what percentage of that group you should feed the iguana. To guarantee optimum health and liveliness, you should vary your pet's diet. It will also affect your iguana's awareness and activity.

GROUP 1: GREENS
(25%–40% OF TOTAL VOLUME)

These are leafy greens, including kale, escarole, mustard greens, collard greens and parsley. In lesser amounts, you might try dandelion greens, romaine lettuce and endive. Spinach should be avoided in the diet, as should beet greens and cabbage. All of these interfere with the body's absorption of calcium.

There is an array of foods on the market to help your iguana expand its taste buds.

48

GROUP 2: BULK VEGETABLES *(25%–40% OF TOTAL VOLUME)*

This group includes peas, carrots, corn, green beans, lima beans and zucchini. In lesser amounts you might also mix in summer squash, avocado and okra. Avoid broccoli, cauliflower and other members of the brassica group. These can bind calcium and cause dietary deficiencies.

GROUP 3: FRUIT *(10% BY VOLUME)*

Pears, peaches, strawberries, blueberries and cantaloupe are excellent food sources. In lesser amounts you might want to try huckleberries, raspberries and apples.

GROUP 4: COMMERCIAL FOODS *(5%–10% BY VOLUME)*

This is a diverse group because of the way that prepared foods are manufactured. Read the labels and be sure that the food you are using does not contain animal material. Because many of these commercial foods are dry, you will want to soak them in water for a while before feeding.

49

CHAPTER SEVEN

Your Iguana's Health

50

The health problems your iguana can develop range from minor to life-threatening. Most require veterinary assistance and some just necessitate an adjustment in husbandry. It is important to be able distinguish the difference between a healthy iguana and one that is ill. Inspect your iguana regularly for signs of good health so you can find the first signs of illness.

The following are conditions you should check for every day.

APPETITE—Does the iguana seem active at mealtime? Does it have a healthy appetite or is it not eating?

BEHAVIOR—Is your iguana unusually quiet? Does it react normally to its surroundings? Is it reacting to you? Is it sluggish?

NOSE—Is there evidence of a discharge around the nose?

*Check your
iguana's body
and behavior
daily.*

51

EYES—Are they sunken into the sockets? Are they swollen? Is there good eye movement? Are the eyes quick and responsive?

MOUTH—Is the mouth open? Is the iguana panting? Is there any mucus or foam or any dried crust around the mouth? Is any part of the mouth or throat swollen?

LIMBS—Are any of the limbs or toes swollen? Are there any toes that have changed color? Is the iguana able to move all of its limbs? Does it walk on all of its limbs? Does it have all of its toes?

SKIN—Are there any cuts on the body or limbs? Are there any unusual discolorations or markings on the skin? Is the crest intact?

SNEEZING—Is your iguana sneezing more than you would expect?

VENT—Is the iguana's vent messy? Is the stool firm or loose? Is your iguana having normal bowel movements? Is it straining?

FINDING A VETERINARIAN

Before you obtain your iguana, it's a very good idea to have a veterinarian already selected. Ask your veterinarian if he or she is a member of the Association of Reptile and Amphibian Veterinarians. This is an organization that informs veterinarians on the latest health information on these types of animals.

Just as there are many different types of pet owners, there are many different types of veterinarians who differ greatly from one another. Some know much about iguanas and some don't. Find a veterinarian who knows quite a bit. You need to be sure that you have a veterinarian who feels comfortable with iguanas and knows the medicine of these animals well.

In a perfect world, we would all live near veterinarians who are knowledgeable about these pets. But, unfortunately, there are almost no courses in veterinary school on iguana medicine. What your veterinarian knows about these pets he or she has learned through reading, attending meetings, experience and dedication. We are not all so fortunate to live in areas where these

Many illnesses can be prevented with good nutrition and a varied diet.

types of veterinarians practice. What do you do if you don't? You find a veterinarian who you trust and make sure that this veterinarian can access the needed reference information on your pet and discuss your pet's health with colleagues.

HEALTH OVERVIEW

There are many different types of diseases and illnesses that can affect your iguana. The most common diseases are those caused by improper husbandry and, sadly, these are the most preventable. These problems usually come from one source: inadequate nutrition.

AN IGUANA GROOMING AND FIRST-AID KIT

It's a good idea to keep a box filled with the necessary materials to care for your iguana. Below is a list of some of the things that would be good to have around.

Antibiotic ointment

Hydrogen peroxide for cleansing/disinfecting

Betadine solution for cleansing/disinfecting

Nail clippers

Gauze for cuts and wounds

Cornstarch to stop minor bleeding

a burn to properly heal. If not attended to, a burn can be fatal.

Burns

This is one of the most common of external accidents and it is completely preventable. Lizards seek out the warmest thing they can and try to get as near to it as possible. Although heat lamps can be placed safely outside the enclosure, heat rocks, placed inside, are a common source of skin burns. Slight burns may heal themselves, but they will leave scars. Serious burns require immediate veterinary attention. It may take many weeks to months for

Lacerations (Cuts)

Lacerations can be caused by a number of objects, including sharp nails or claws; scratches or bites from another iguana; or rubbing against something sharp in the enclosure. These wounds may vary in their seriousness, ranging from abrasions to deep cuts. These need to be addressed immediately. For anything more serious than an abrasion, you need to seek a veterinarian's help. If it is possible to cleanse

53

the wound without harming the iguana and harming yourself, you can use clean water to douse the wound. Do not use Band-Aids or adhesive strips of any kind. Deep lacerations are very serious problems, considered emergencies, and need to be seen by a doctor as soon as possible.

Nose Rubbing

This is one of the most common ailments iguanas suffer, due to poor husbandry and your iguana's need to explore. Iguanas will rub the skin right off of their snouts. If this is not treated quickly and earnestly, it may require surgery and leave your iguana scarred for life. Most of the time, it is a result of a cage or enclosure that is too small or too cluttered for the iguana. It can also be a sign that there is inadequate light or heat and the iguana is trying to get to a warmer area.

Iguanas rub their noses against the walls or top of the cage in an effort to escape. If you have a wire cage, you may want to replace it with plastic-coated fine wire mesh, which will reduce rostral abrasions. Make as many changes to the enclosure as necessary, as it is the only long-term cure.

Make sure that when you first notice the swelling and the rawness of the snout, you remove your iguana from the enclosure and make appropriate husbandry changes. Wash the abrasion, and coat it with an antibiotic ointment. Change the environment around the enclosure in any way you can to make your pet happier. Treat the snout for a few days, and watch your pet closely. If the wound does not heal within a few days, contact your veterinarian.

Keep your iguana housed in a cage with ample room for it to roam.

Toe or Nail Disorders

Most broken or torn toes or nails are the result of an iguana's getting its claws stuck in something. It will pull and twist until its toe either becomes disjointed, a nail snaps off or it breaks the toe.

Broken Limbs

When a long bone of the leg or arm is broken, it is usually the result of an accident or the first sign of metabolic bone disease. Iguanas are built to take some serious punishment in the wild and are very active, especially when they feel frightened or threatened. Excellent swimmers and runners, they can jump, swim and run at blinding speeds. So, it is unusual for your iguana to break its bones with normal activity. If your iguana fractures one of its limbs without an accident occurring, then the cause of the break is probably a metabolic bone disorder.

Broken bones need to be attended to by a veterinarian as soon as possible. If the break is due to an accident, your veterinarian will recommend a plan of treatment. Most likely, x-rays will be taken to see how serious the break is. Then your

HOME CARE FOR THE ILL IGUANA

There are four things you must remember when dealing with an ill or recuperating iguana:

1. Don't handle your iguana at this time. Iguanas find contact stressful. By touching your iguana as a means of consoling it, you will achieve just the opposite effect, as it stresses from the contact.

2. Make sure to raise the temperature of the basking site within the enclosure. Warmth will always help an ailing iguana. Also, maintain a cooling-off place where the iguana can go when it is too hot.

3. Rehydration is very important. Many iguanas become dehydrated when ill. Fine misting and bathing will help your sick iguana.

4. Stay in contact with your veterinarian. This is the most important thing you can do for the health of your iguana.

doctor will recommend the best way to treat it, whether it be confinement, a splint or surgery. Broken bones caused by metabolic bone disease, which results from nutritional deficiency, are treated differently— correction of the husbandry problems being the first priority.

55

Broken Tails

In nature, the iguana, like other lizards, has some excellent defense mechanisms. One of them involves the tail. When attacked by predators, iguanas are sometimes caught by the tail. Luckily enough, an iguana's tail is meant to break. There are even special places in the tailbones that are meant to break, if needed, so that when a predator catches the iguana by the tail, the tail breaks loose from the body and the iguana runs away while the predator is left with a tail in its mouth. The appendage will continue to wiggle and writhe, thus holding the attention of the predator while the iguana makes its escape. So, if for some reason your iguana loses its tail, do not be upset; the iguana may grow a new tail! If your iguana loses most of its tail, it may not grow all of it back. The shorter the piece of the tail it loses, the better the chances it will all grow back.

Depending on the type of break, there may be no urgency involved regarding seeking medical care. As long as the break occurs on the last third of the tail, little bleeding will occur and regeneration of a new tail

An iguana's tail was designed to break and regrow—but don't play rough with it!

Keeping an iguana's skin moist is the best way to facilitate shedding.

will begin almost immediately. If the break occurs near the tail base, the iguana will require immediate veterinary attention. This is considered a wound and must be cauterized quickly in order to avoid massive bleeding and infection.

Be forewarned: There is little you can do to help in the regeneration of your pet's tail. Many times the tail will grow back thicker and shorter and a different color. Almost always, the second tail will never be as long, thin and whiplike as the first. Some iguanas have even been known to grow a forked tail during regeneration.

Improper Shedding

What is improper shedding? Sometimes the skin does not come off readily. This is especially true of the skin around the toes. If the skin on a toe becomes wrapped tightly, one end of the toe may become incredibly swollen. If this problem is not addressed, your iguana will probably lose that toe. It is important that when shedding begins you pay extra special attention to your pet's toes. Don't try to peel off skin that isn't ready to come off.

Iguanas shed as they grow and will not shed their entire skin the way most snakes do. Also unlike snakes that shed in one piece, iguanas shed in many pieces. This is normal. But in time, all areas of the body should have new skin. If there is an area that never sheds, this needs veterinary attention.

One of the best ways to facilitate shedding is to bathe your iguana at the time shedding is taking place. A bath in lukewarm water will help to soften up the skin and allow it to come off more easily. Also, daily misting will help with a problem shed. (See chapter 8 for more information on bathing and misting.)

A Word on Salmonella

It is best to assume that your iguana carries in its intestines the bacteria salmonella, which can live there harmlessly or may cause a disease like diarrhea. Even without signs of disease, salmonella can be in the stool of your iguana, and a person who does not practice proper hygiene may contract some of these salmonella bacteria.

Proper hygiene means never allowing anything that has contacted iguana feces to contact anything that will enter a person's mouth. That means washing your hands whenever you touch your iguana, especially if you are eating or preparing food. If your iguana roams around your house, make sure it does not enter food preparation areas. And if it defecates in the house, make sure you clean it up thoroughly with a cleaning agent, such as bleach.

One must be especially vigilant with children and iguanas. Children are always putting their hands in their mouths, and do not realize the dangers of salmonella. It is important to teach children to thoroughly wash their hands after handling their pet iguana.

DIAGNOSING SALMONELLA

It is not easy to diagnose salmonella disease in your iguana. Your veterinarian can do a fecal culture, but even if it is negative for salmonella, your iguana can still be silently harboring the bacteria. And if it is positive for salmonella, it does not necessarily mean that salmonella is making your iguana sick.

There are millions of examples of people who have had reptiles as pets who have never gotten sick with salmonella. Yes, salmonella is a serious disease, but with proper hygiene it is totally preventable.

Remember, it is more common to get salmonella from improperly cooked meat or eggs than from your pet iguana.

Metabolic Bone Disease (MBD)

Metabolic bone disease is the most common and preventable disease in iguanas. Most cases of MBD are seen in young iguanas, but it is also seen in female iguanas who are producing eggs but are not being supplemented properly.

Metabolic bone disease is a husbandry problem caused by malnutrition or overall improper care of an iguana. An iguana must have the correct nutrients, plenty of heat and lots of ultraviolet light. An environment lacking in any of these three required components can result in MBD.

One of the first signs of MBD in your iguana is found on the face, especially the jaw. It feels rubbery and will develop a series of swellings or lumps. You can actually squeeze the jawbone when pinched together. Bones should be strong. The other bones will soon start to be affected, too. First, they may become swollen, almost giving a Popeye appearance

to the bones—the forearms may be extremely thick and much heavier than the rest of the leg. This may make the iguana look, to the inexperienced eye, as if it were fat and healthy. Actually, the swelling is the body's attempt to compensate for the lack of calcium.

As the disease progresses, bones in this condition are apt to break, including the bones of the spine. The head may become misshapen, as the upper and lower jaws don't come together properly. Sometimes a tail that breaks off too easily is the first sign of MBD.

You must seek out a veterinarian immediately.

The good news is that the changes caused by MBD are

An environment lacking nutrients, heat and ultraviolet light can cause metabolic bone disease in your iguana.

59

Because the iguana spends so much time in the heat, it is important to keep it hydrated.

reversible if caught early enough. Many iguanas go on to live a healthy, normal life. If caught too late, the iguana may end up with deformities, especially a broken back, that affects its daily life.

Metabolic bone disease is also seen in female iguanas that have poor husbandry or a marginally good diet. Female iguanas that are producing eggs need extra nutrients to compensate for all that their body requires to produce those eggs. (Remember, a female iguana doesn't need a male around to produce eggs.) When a female has

to start using its bone stores of calcium to make eggs, the bones become soft.

If your female iguana starts laying eggs, please contact your veterinarian to make sure that its diet is adequate, especially in terms of calcium, to prevent MBD. It is always much easier to prevent a disease than cure it once it occurs.

Kidney Disease

Kidney disease is most common in young to middle-age iguanas (3 to 5 years old) and seems to hit the large, fast-growing iguanas that appear nice and healthy on the outside— that is, until they get sick. Also, many of these fast-growing iguanas are fed animal protein while doing their growing.

If your iguana develops kidney disease, it will become lethargic, stop eating, maybe change color and lose weight. If you start seeing these signs, take your pet to the veterinarian as soon as possible.

The Stools

HEALTHY
The consistency of your iguana's stool will tell you a lot about its

health. If the stool is sort of jelly-like, with a white, milky finish, you have a healthy iguana. If it's hard and dry, then you have a sick iguana. A healthy iguana is also very regular.

The best way to keep your iguana regular is to provide it with a proper diet with lots of vegetable fiber, plenty of water, heat and light. The iguana needs water to hydrate its system. The sun and the heat help the iguana's digestion system function properly.

Iguanas typically have one vent movement per day. Usually they dispose of these wastes in the same place, so as to keep the rest of their living area clean. Most often, they discard their excesses in their water bowl.

DIARRHEA

Any number of disorders can cause a temporary case of diarrhea in an iguana. Stress is the most common factor. A change in diet is another main reason. Diarrhea can also be brought on by infections by bacteria, protozoa, nematodes and other parasites.

For the first day or so, try to change your iguana's diet to firm up its stool, supplementing its usual meals with fiber-rich foods. If the diarrhea does not improve after two days of treatment, you will need to consult with your veterinarian.

CONSTIPATION

Iguanas suffering from constipation may become lethargic. They will appear bloated. Their actions and reactions will be much slower than usual. They may appear to strain and try to defecate but nothing comes out. One cause is a lack of hydration. Without proper amounts of water, the iguana cannot pass its waste and the intestines will become impacted. Another common cause is the lack of proper environmental temperature and the lack of a proper diet.

Iguanas with MBD usually become constipated due to a lack of calcium, which allows the intestines to work properly. Finally, an iguana kept on a dirt or gravel substrate can eat this material, causing a blockage and constipation. Mild cases may respond to water baths. This will usually cause them to pass their waste. Make sure not to put your pet's head under the water.

More serious cases should be brought immediately to your veterinarian.

Endoparasitic Problems

These include protozoa, pinworms, roundworms, tapeworms and flukes. Whenever your iguana has diarrhea or a watery stool consistently, one of the above parasites must be considered as a cause. Many iguanas are routinely dewormed before they are sold. It is important to remember that iguanas depend on some of these organisms to help them properly digest their foods. But sometimes these parasites, or others, grow in too great an amount for your iguana's system to hold them in check.

To detect these organisms, a fecal examination should be done on your iguana by your veterinarian.

Mites

These are the most common ectoparasitic problems that confront iguanas. Mites are not always easy to find. You have to look hard to see them. They live on and off of your iguana. Sometimes the skin infected with mites will turn black and blotchy. More than just an annoyance, mites can carry disease. Mites are not so easy to cure, and sometimes the cure is also harmful to your pet. There may be many products on the shelf of your pet store to cure mites, but it is better to contact your veterinarian before doing anything. You need to treat both your pet and the area it lives in. Your veterinarian has safe ways of curing your pet of this condition.

Ticks

Like in other animals, an iguana's ticks need to be removed carefully. They look like little black and brown seeds attached to your iguana's body. Sometimes they are small and flat—that's how you know that they are relatively new—and sometimes they are big and roundish, which means they've been feeding for a while.

Make sure to dab the tick with rubbing alcohol and let it sit for just a few minutes before removing it. Then, with a pair of tweezers, gently remove it. The objective with a tick, as always, is to make sure you get the whole tick and not just the body.

If you are not sure you can do this, please go see your veterinarian.

Respiratory Problems

Just like you, the iguana can get a respiratory infection. This usually occurs in stressed iguanas, such as those recently imported or those with improper husbandry conditions. It is very common in iguanas that are kept too cold. How can you tell if your iguana has a respiratory problem? It will act just like you do when you have a cold: It will lose its appetite, sneeze, have a runny nose and lack energy and may even breathe very hard. Keep in mind that iguanas have salt glands in their noses that they routinely empty by "sneezing," which is normal and does not indicate a respiratory infection. A sure sign of a respiratory problem is fluid or mucus bubbling from the nose.

The best thing you can do before you see the veterinarian is to supply plenty of water and make sure you increase the temperature of the hot zone in the enclosure, as this will hopefully strengthen the bodily processes in your iguana. If you live in a relatively cool area, especially the north, damp cold can be an iguana's worst enemy. Make sure you have sufficient heating twenty-four hours a day.

Reproductive Problems

Both the males and the females have reproductive problems that necessitate visits to the veterinarian. The male iguana has two hemipenes, which are part of his reproductive system. Sometimes the male will injure himself and damage one or both of his hemipenes. Sometimes the hemipenes prolapse, meaning they come out of their sac in the area along the tail near the vent and can't be replaced. If not treated swiftly and properly, a problem like this could result in the loss of one of these hemipenes.

Females produce eggs even without the presence of a male iguana and they need to lay them. If they don't have proper nutrients, they won't be able to lay their eggs. Female iguanas will hold their eggs if they can't find a suitable place to lay them. This is a problem in captivity, as they mostly bury their eggs in warm, deep dirt. When such a place isn't available, they hold on to

63

You can prevent your female iguana from developing serious medical problems by spaying her.

Neutering Your Iguana

In female iguanas, spaying prevents them from becoming egg-bound, which is a medical problem. Female iguanas go through egg production each year whether or not they have mated, and each time they do they are prone to binding and calcium deficiency. These are serious medical problems that can be totally prevented by removing the ovaries and oviduct (spaying). This procedure should be done by an experienced veterinarian.

the eggs, eventually causing an illness called retained eggs.

The condition of retained eggs is recognized by the fact that your female iguana will develop an enlarged abdomen and become lethargic. Again, though some literature will recommend home remedies and other possible drugs toxic to your iguana to help her expel the eggs, this is not a course of action that should be attempted. The eggs must be removed by an experienced veterinarian, the sooner the better.

In males, neutering (removing the testes) is not a common procedure. This is because there is no medical reason to do this. When people want their male iguana neutered, it is for behavioral reasons. Male iguanas can be very aggressive toward other iguanas and their owners. A once sweet, easy-to-handle male iguana may turn into a tail-swishing, person-chasing reptile who actually poses a risk to his owners. Veterinarians have neutered these aggressive males in an attempt to stop this sexually related behavior.

Recently, veterinarians have been neutering male iguanas before they become sexually mature to see if this procedure done early in life decreases male sexual aggressiveness. The jury is still out as to whether this is going to be a successful way to curb this problem. As with females, neutering of male iguanas should only be done by a veterinarian experienced in these procedures.

Male Heat

Once a year, some dominant males will get into what some people call "male heat." This is a temporary condition, which generally lasts two months depending on the area of the country you are in. This behavior is due to the dominant male's aggressive personality and sexual assertiveness.

Many owners interpret this activity to mean that their animal is turning against them, but this is not the case. Aggressive iguanas strike quickly; the male in heat will simply move more deliberately to satisfy itself.

What happens to a male iguana during the breeding season? This only happens to some males—those that are particularly dominant and territorial. They become especially restless, often pacing around their cage or a room. This is because the territorial instinct becomes even stronger when the mating instinct hits.

These males will try to find a substitute if they cannot mate a female. The substitute could be your finger, arm or leg, and it doesn't matter whether you are a man or a woman. This is very alarming, especially if you're caught unaware.

Between iguanas, if the female tries to escape from the male, she increases his efforts to hold on to her. The same thing will happen if you try to quickly separate yourself from your iguana. The best thing to do is push your fingers against the iguana's eyes—not so hard that you cause serious harm, but enough to cause some distracting pain.

The breeding season lasts two to three months, during the tropical, rainy season in the summer. During this time, it's best to avoid handling your male, and keep it separated from other iguanas.

CHAPTER EIGHT

Grooming the Iguana

Aside from trimming its claws, there is little to grooming an iguana. It may need a daily light misting or bathing, but that's it.

GENERAL APPEARANCE

The healthy iguana's skin should be clean and smooth with a healthy sheen. The skin color may gradually change over time—the key word being gradually. Any sudden color variations should be inspected and investigated by your veterinarian at once. In a healthy iguana, the eyes fill the sockets, the animal has a healthy appetite and there should be no bloating or swelling in any of the limbs or belly.

You will find that your iguana welcomes baths after basking.

67

BATHING

Most iguanas love to swim and take a bath. It is easier to start this routine early in life rather than when your iguana is an adult. If you bathe your iguana, make sure that it dries off properly so that it doesn't get chilled.

To bathe your iguana, simply put a large bowl of lukewarm water in the enclosure with the iguana. Your iguana, hopefully, will climb right in and do its thing. Do this at least once a week.

The purpose of a good bath is to clean the iguana and loosen up any skin that might be ready to come off, as iguanas do shed their skin. Also, this gives your iguana something fun to do! Leave the water in the enclosure for two to three hours, then remove it and leave plenty of time for the iguana to dry off. It's that simple.

Some people will put their iguana into the tub to let it swim. This is not recommended because of the possibility that your iguana could shed the salmonella bacteria in the tub. Whoever uses the tub next would be exposed to this bacteria, which can lead to severe illness or even death in humans. Although

GROOMING YOUR IGUANA

You wouldn't think so, but grooming your iguana will be a lot like grooming your cat or dog! Here's what you'll need to do regularly:

- **Clip nails:** Left untended, your iguana's nails will grow long and sharp. Such nails can hurt you or your iguana by tearing skin; they can also get stuck in fabric or wire meshing, causing the iguana to risk injury by struggling to free itself.

- **Give a bath:** Iguanas love water, and besides taking short swims in their water bowls, should be allowed to swim in a large container of water at least once a week. They also like to be misted.

- **Tend to shedding skin:** Yes, iguanas shed—just like your furry friends! They shed their skin into pieces, and you may need to help remove these occasionally. You'll certainly need to remove dead skin from the iguana's environment.

- **Pay attention to overall condition:** Keep an eye on your iguana's skin, noting color and texture. Recognize what's healthy so you'll know when something's off.

- **Keep it clean:** Don't let a small problem become a big one by letting general grooming and hygiene slip. Keep your iguana and its cage clean.

you can disinfect the tub against salmonella, it is best to always be on the safe side and not let your iguana swim in the tub.

MISTING

Once a day, spray the iguana's enclosure using water in a small spray bottle with a mist nozzle. Do not aim the bottle directly at the iguana. Rather, aim it up, so that the mist falls like rain onto the enclosure and the iguana. Make sure the spray is as fine as it can be.

SKIN DARKENING

Sometimes, when iguanas are basking during the day, they begin to turn a darker color, sometimes black. This will only happen for brief periods. Iguanas also turn darker when they are cold. It's only when your iguana turns pale or suddenly changes to colors like orange or yellow that you need to worry and seek the help of a qualified veterinarian.

SNEEZING

Iguanas possess special organs called nasal salt glands. To empty these

Its claws are the iguana's best weapons, and they will grow long and dangerous if left unclipped.

glands, they sneeze. When the animal sneezes, it is expelling salt from its passages. This is very healthy.

CLIPPING CLAWS

This is an important grooming technique to master. If not done regularly, your iguana will eventually injure itself, maybe another iguana and possibly you—all quite unintentionally with nails that are too long.

In nature, the iguana's claws grow long and sharp, and are its best weapons, whether facing another iguana or another species. They can use these claws to help climb trees. These claws can be long, thin and razor sharp, and do lots of damage. The trimming of claws should be done on a regular basis.

You will need three things to do the job correctly: good restraint, clippers and some kind of clotting agent. Nail clippers for cats or birds will do fine for iguanas, and can be purchased at any pet shop. A clotting agent, like Kwik Stop or common cornstarch, is necessary in case the nail is trimmed too far down and starts to bleed. Restraint depends on your iguana and your ability to hold your pet.

When trimming the nails of any pet, it is important to cut off only the sharp tips. Inside each nail is a

The first time this happens you will feel horrible. The animal obviously feels pain, and of course you feel bad because you have hurt your pet. Make sure you jump back on the horse, though. If you give up after that, it will take you forever to get back to it. Just trim the nails carefully, and make sure your working area is extremely well lit so you can see what you are doing.

Doing the Clipping

To properly cut the nails of an iguana, there should ideally be two people. Both of you will hold the iguana down; one person at the head and throat and the other holding the back legs and the base of the tail.

It is very helpful to wrap the animal in a towel, leaving only the claw to be cut exposed. The iguana seems to feel safer in this situation. It is important to make sure your iguana is calm and you do not fight with it too much. You must remember that grooming is all part of handling.

Hold the iguana's digit in your hand. Especially in young iguanas, the quick will be visible as a thin red

Your iguana's aquarium is a breeding ground for bacteria. It is necessary to keep your pet's environment fresh and to clean the aquarium out weekly, if not more often.

blood vessel called the quick. The quick extends through the body of the nail but ends before the tip of the nail. If you cut too much of the nail off, the iguana will most definitely flinch and blood will appear. It is important at that point to rub the coagulant into the nail quickly. If left open, the wound, especially in an iguana, could lead to serious infection. The bleeding should stop within a minute.

Again, only cut the sharpest end off. If you cut the quick too often, your iguana will resist handling at any time and you'll end up with a bloody mess every time. And it is painful to the iguana.

or black line running down the inside of the claw. Then, carefully, clip off the sharpest point—just the tip of the nail.

GENERAL MAINTENANCE

The enclosure should be cleaned at least weekly. The water should be changed daily. If you have an aquarium, empty it out and clean all the sides. Also, replace the substrate and make sure the entire area is clean. An unclean area will wear down the immune system of an otherwise healthy iguana.

As a result of sunbathing, the iguana's skin can turn a darker color for brief periods.

71

CHAPTER NINE

Iguanas in the Wild

With the rise in popularity of the iguana, more people want to see these magnificent creatures in their natural habitat. And they want other people to see their iguana. This chapter discusses satisfying both urges, whether you want to travel to see iguanas in the wild, or whether you want to train your iguana to brave the wild world with you.

SEEING IGUANAS IN THE WILD

Though many of the most beautiful iguanas come from Central America, including countries like Mexico, Honduras and Costa Rica, and even Puerto Rico, the Bahamas and other Caribbean islands, the iguana can also be found somewhat closer to home in the United States.

The green iguana can be found in states with hot climates, wetlands and lush vegetation, like Florida.

73

As was previously mentioned, iguanas have been bred and released in places like Florida, which have weather patterns similar to the iguanas' native habitat. And in these places they are thriving. Of course, there have always been Chuckwallas in Texas, New Mexico and Arizona, and they can be found in abundance along canyons and roadsides throughout the Southwest.

FLORIDA AND TEXAS

In these hot states, green iguanas can be found in numerous wetlands and parks, abiding anywhere where there is running water and trees. Water is a life necessity and is usually found where there is also food and protection. The same goes for the trees. Strange as it may seem, many iguanas have been found in the wooded areas around Miami's International Airport and in some of the suburbs surrounding the airport. But generally speaking, the more remote the area is from human beings, the more likely you are to find a number of green iguanas. Iguanas of 5 and 6 feet in length have been reported in these areas.

When you're doing your iguana-watching, move quietly and make sure you pack a pair of binoculars

CAPTURING WILD IGUANAS

Do not attempt to capture one of these animals. Removing them from their natural habitat is illegal and prosecutable under the law. Also, many of these animals, having had the freedom to roam vast areas of ground, would make unhappy captives. Why take the risk, and why make a beautiful, wild iguana miserable?

and a camera with a telephoto lens. You are not going to get too close to any of these animals. Before entering private property to see an iguana, ask permission. Trespassing is a serious offense, and you may be prosecuted. Always make sure of where you are and that the owner knows you're there.

THE GREAT SOUTHWEST

This is home to America's native-born Chuckwalla. Experts disagree about the number of varieties of Chuckwallas that exist, but Chuckwallas generally are black and brick-red in color, and some have cream-colored tails.

You can find Chuckwallas anywhere in the Southwest where there are creosote plants. Although Chuckwallas tend to eat insects and other prey, they are mainly vegetarians. Rivers or canyons will be home to these large animals.

Ranging all the way from Utah to Nevada, Arizona, New Mexico and Texas, you can find these big chubby characters in abundance. They tend to sit on ledges or other rocks during the day. Make no mistake, though: They will see you long before you see them. Again, you won't ever get too close to them.

With their large bellies, thick, short tails and lack of spines along the back, these are not as interesting looking as green iguanas. They are desert creatures, whose colorings blend better with the landscape than the green iguana. It is fascinating to see these fat but nimble creatures quickly navigate the arid landscape, using the crevices in rocks to save themselves from predators.

You can find these animals almost anywhere in the Southwest. When you're driving on the roads in these states, all you need to do is keep a keen eye trained on the landscape. Once you spot a couple, you'll begin to pick them out of the landscape immediately.

TEXAS AND MEXICO

The desert iguana is a common sight in these places, though it is by far the smallest of the iguana family. Growing an average of only 12 to 18 inches long, this tan and gray slim lizard is fast and agile. Like the Chuckwalla, the desert iguana lacks the large scaly mane of the green iguana. The desert iguana inhabits much of the same territory as the Chuckwalla and can be found in many of the same areas.

According to iguana enthusiasts, the desert iguana is especially plentiful in Imperial and San Diego counties. Those large, duned areas sport a variety of these sleek little lizards darting through the sandy terrain. Unlike the Chuckwalla and the green iguana, the desert iguana is an accomplished burrow dweller. It can dig a deep burrow quick enough to enable its escape from predators.

The green iguana can be found in states with hot climates, wetlands and lush vegetation, like Florida.

This young spiny-tailed iguana flourishes in climates typical of Mexico and Panama.

The desert iguana is sometimes hard to see in its native habitat because it blends in with the environment so well.

75

CHAPTER TEN

Complete Listing of Iguanas

Although the green iguana is the most popular pet of the iguanid family, there are in fact eight genera in this family, each with their own species. These iguanids have very different sizes, types and colorations. They are presented here for the iguana enthusiast.

The descriptions of the family of *Iguanidae* are taken from various sources, including R. D. and Patricia P. Bartlett's book *Iguanas,* and Frank Slaven's book *Reptiles and Amphibians in Captivity.*

AMBLYRHYNCHUS CRISTATUS—GALAPAGOS MARINE IGUANA

Listed as CITES (Convention on the International Trade of Endangered Species) Appendix I, this is a protected species. The Galapagos marine iguana was described by Charles Darwin on his trip to the Galapagos Islands. This species is at least a foot shorter than the green iguana, growing to a length of about 5 feet. There are several types of Galapagos marine iguanas, all peculiar to the island they live on. They have a very special diet. Because these lizards eat fresh seaweed and ocean algae, they are a very difficult species to keep in captivity, which is why none are known to be within the United States. They are the only marine lizard in the world, diving in and out of the pounding surf for their diet. They have the ability to do this because of a special gland that secretes the salt out through the nostrils. They are excellent swimmers. While they do display bright red patches during the mating season, they are normally a brown and gray color.

BRACHYLOPHUS SPP

BRACHYLOPHUS SPP—FIJI IGUANA There are actually two species in this genera and they are found on the Fiji and Tonga islands. Both are endangered, which has garnered them a CITES Appendix I rating. There have been encouraging results via protection and captive breeding in Fiji and in the United States, including at the San Diego, Dallas, Fresno and Cincinnati zoos. Fiji iguanas are very small in length and the males rarely average more than 2½ feet in length, including the tail. The females are shorter. These iguanas are usually not available to the hobbyist through any legitimate means.

BRACHYLOPHUS FASCIATUS— FIJI BANDED IGUANA This is certainly one of the most beautiful reptiles on earth. The males are colorfully marked with alternating green and light-blue bands. The females are entirely green.

BRACHYLOPHUS VITIENSIS— FIJI CRESTED IGUANA This is an animal very similar to the Fiji banded iguana; however, as the name indicates, the crest at the nuchal area (just behind the head) is substantially higher and more pronounced.

CONOLOPHUS SPP

CONOLOPHUS SPP—GALAPAGOS LAND IGUANA These are also listed under CITES Appendix I. Unlike the marine iguana, the land iguana stays solely on land, and as is true of many of the *Iguanadae* family, is an accomplished tree climber. It eats shoots, flowers, fruits, cactus pads and grasshoppers. It may grow up to 4 feet in length, and females are slightly shorter than males.

Listed below are two species of the Galapagos land iguana, though some experts would argue that *Conolophus pallidus* and *C. subcristatus* are the same species. These lizards are rarely seen outside of their native regions. They tend to be a yellowish-brown color.

**CONOLOPHUS SUBCRISTATUS—
GALAPAGOS LAND IGUANA**
This is the better known of the two species.

**CONOLOPHUS PALLIDUS—
GALAPAGOS LAND IGUANA**
This may be the same species as C. subcristatus.

CTENOSAURA SPP

Found from Mexico to Panama and on some Colombian islands, the Ctenosaura genera includes nine species. Known as spiny-tailed or black iguanas, they are commonly available, and some of the rarer species are being bred on farms in several countries. Some are affordable even to the beginning hobbyist. Some zoologists do not recognize *Enyliosaurus* species as an iguana, but it is listed for the sake of completeness.

This group, especially as they become adults, tends not to be brightly colored, although there are exceptions. The thing that differentiates them from other iguanas is the spiny tail. The tail is noted for the winding, sharp, raised scales that protrude from it. Mature adults use this tail as a rather intimidating weapon.

Few of the *Ctenosaura* species grow beyond 3 feet in length and, as is true of other genera, the females tend to be slightly shorter than the males. Many of these lizards are imported, but captive breeding, especially in the United States, is increasing the availability of these species.

**CTENOSAURA ACANTHURA—
SPINY-TAILED IGUANA OR
BLACK IGUANA** Averaging more than 3 feet in length, this species is found abundantly along Mexico's Gulf Coast and in some areas of Central America. This species is more terrestrial than arboreal. Some experts believe that this species is closely related to the *C. hemilopha.*

**CTENOSAURA BAKERI—ISLA DE
LA BAHIA SPINY-TAILED
IGUANA** Hailing from an island off of Honduras, little is known about this extremely rare reptile. No zoo or private collector is known to possess one of these iguanids.

CTENOSAURA (ENYLIOSAURUS) CLARKI—MICHOACAN (CLARK'S) DWARF SPINY-TAILED IGUANA Protected by the Mexican government, several specimens are found in zoos and private collections. This species is closely related to *Ctenosaura defensor,* but it is less brightly colored. The average length in males does not exceed 1 foot and females are slightly smaller.

CTENOSAURA (ENYLIOSAURUS) DEFENSOR—YUCATÁN DWARF SPINY-TAILED IGUANA This is another small iguanid. As the name indicates, this animal is found on the Yucatán Peninsula in Mexico. It is plentiful in its natural habitat. This is perhaps the most colorful of the entire *Ctenosaura* genera, with bands of black, blue, red, orange and yellow across its back.

CTENOSAURA HEMILOPHA—SONORAN SPINY-TAILED IGUANA One of the larger *Ctenosaura,* the Sonoran can grow up to 3 feet in length, and its spiky tail usually accounts for more than half of that length. They are quite common in the Baja California Sur area and in the northwest region of Mexico. It is darkly colored and has a stocky body shape.

CTENOSAURA OEIRHINA—ROATAN ISLAND SPINY-TAILED IGUANA Very much like the Isla de la Bahia iguana, this small iguana comes from an isolated island off the coast of Honduras. The movement of these animals is restricted and few are known to exist outside of their natural habitat. Little is known about their natural history.

CTENOSAURA (ENYLIOSAURUS) PALERIS—CENTRAL AMERICAN DWARF SPINY-TAILED IGUANA Sometimes referred to as the Honduran dwarf spiny-tailed iguana, this reptile is quite commonly found in Guatemala and Honduras. They may grow to be a little over 1 foot in length and the females are somewhat shorter. They are in the collections of several zoos. They are found in semiarid conditions.

CTENOSAURA PECTINATA—MEXICAN SPINY-TAILED IGUANA This is the largest of the *Ctenosaura* genera, measuring up to 4 feet in length. Recently transplanted to Florida and Texas, this reptile is native to the Pacific

Mexican coast. This species is available to the pet trade. The Mexican spiny-tailed iguana is an excellent example of how environmentalists and trade hobbyists can best work together, as many farms have increased the size of this population to the point that this species is now sold in the trade. This iguana's coloring is dark gray with either yellow or white bands. It is seen in many zoological collections including the Indianapolis, Los Angeles and Bronx zoos.

CTENOSAURA (ENYLIOSAURUS) QUINQUECARTINATA—DWARF SPINY-TAILED IGUANA OR THE CLUB-TAILED IGUANA   This is the largest of the dwarf iguanas, a dubious distinction, as it routinely measures little more than 12 to 15 inches in length. It is found in southern Mexico and areas of Nicaragua. It has recently become available to the pet trade.

CTENOSAURA SIMILIS—SPINY-TAILED IGUANA   This species is very similar to *C. acanthura*, except that although the black iguana ranges from the southwestern United States and northern Mexico, this species ranges from southwest-

ern Mexico all the way to Panama. The colorings tend to be more vivid than other iguanids, with black, green and yellow markings. Averaging more than 3 feet in length, this species is very healthy and is occasionally available to the pet trade.

CYCLURAE

These fourteen species of iguanas are much larger than the common green iguana. There are many variations of this particular group, the largest subset of the iguana family. The species listed under this heading have CITES Appendix I status and are protected by international law. These animals are prohibited from international trade. On the very rare occasion when they are legally offered for sale, they have been bred in captivity by professionals. Although they are extremely handsome lizards, they are also very expensive.

CYCLURA CARINATA BARTSCHI—BOOBY CAY (BARTSCHI'S) ROCK IGUANA   This is a highly threatened species, and enjoys protection under CITES Appendix II. Among the rarest of iguanas, the Bartletts report that fewer than 300 of these animals are known to exist in a small area known as Booby Cay in the Bahama Islands.

CYCLURA CARINATA CARINATA—TURKS ISLAND IGUANA OR CAICOS ISLAND IGUANA

Ranging about 2 feet in length, these reptiles are known to live on Turks Island and Caicos Island off the Bahamas. They look very similar to the rhinoceros iguana, but are smaller. They have a much larger population than the Booby Cay iguana, but are threatened nonetheless.

CYCLURA COLLEI—JAMAICAN ROCK IGUANA

It was thought that this group of iguana was extinct; however, the Bartletts report that this species was rediscovered in 1990. Probably fewer than 100 specimens are alive at this time. They tend to grow about 3½ feet in length and females are slightly shorter than males. There are a few in captivity in Jamaica, but none are known to exist outside of that country.

CYCLURA CORNUTA CORNUTA—RHINOCEROS IGUANA OR HISPANIOLA RHINOCEROS IGUANA

This is the most common and largest lizard of the Cyclura genera. Some easily become domesticated and accepting of human companionship, but most will not. These iguanas are known for having a nasty bite, so watch out! They are considered fairly intelligent and can even differentiate their owner from other humans. These are very handsome iguanas.

The males are almost 4 feet in length and are very stocky animals, being the heaviest of all the iguana family. Some weigh up to 20 pounds! This iguana gets the name "rhinoceros" from the conical growths on top of its snout, which are more pronounced on females than on males. It is found in zoo collections throughout the world.

CYCLURA CORNUTA ONCHIOPPSIS—NAVASSA ISLANDS RHINOCEROS IGUANA

Thought to be extinct, this smaller version of the rhinoceros iguana is native to the small islands off the coast of Haiti.

81

CYCLURA CORNUTA STEJNEGERI—MONA ISLAND RHINOCEROS IGUANA

This iguana takes its name from the tiny Puerto Rican island from which it comes. It is thought that fewer than 3,000 specimens remain. Few zoos have extant specimens, and no private collectors acknowledge possession of this species.

CYCLURA CYCHLURA CYCHLURA—ANDROS ISLAND ROCK IGUANA

This specimen is unique to the Andros Island, a small island in the Bahamas. Even though this species is more plentiful in the wild than many other *Cyclura* species, they are still endangered. They range from 3 to 3½ feet in length. This group is unique as the females grow to approximately the same length as the males.

CYCLURA CYCHLURA FIGGINSI—EXUMA ISLAND ROCK IGUANA

This iguana is found on the Exuma Cays of the Bahama Islands. The average length is thought to be less than 30 inches. Only about 1,500 of these specimens are thought to exist at this time.

CYCLURA CYCHLURA INORNATA—ALLEN'S CAY ROCK IGUANA

This iguana, though not brightly colored, is actually one of the more interesting of the iguanids. It has dark brownish-grayish coloring except on the head. The head is usually a light gray to white. Another of the Bahama iguanas, it grows to be a little less than 3 feet in length and is extremely endangered.

CYCLURA NUBILIA CAYMENENSIS—CAYMAN ISLAND ROCK IGUANA OR LITTLE CAYMAN ROCK IGUANA

This species resembles its close cousin, the Grand Cayman Island rock iguana, in the sense that the males tend to be more docile and slightly shorter. They generally grow a little over 3 feet in length. Less than 1,500 of these animals exist and have CITES Appendix II protection status.

CYCLURA NUBILA LEWSI—GRAND CAYMAN ROCK IGUANA

These are among the most beautiful of all iguanas as they are a lovely shade of aqua-blue. As in all of the *C. nubilia* subspecies, the males tend to be less aggressive than the females. These iguanas are only slightly shorter than the *C. cornuta*. Fewer than 500 of these animals are thought to be alive. Professionals in the Bahamas and the United States have begun breeding these animals in captivity in an attempt to save them from extinction.

CYCLURA NUBILIA NUBILIA— CUBAN ROCK IGUANA This is the second most common subspecies of this group. The Cuban rock iguana is the largest of the rhinoceros iguanas, reaching up to 5 feet in length. This iguana is also being professionally bred and is available to hobbyists. It originates from Cuba but was introduced years ago to Puerto Rico.

CYCLURA PINGUIS—ANEGADA ISLAND ROCK IGUANA This iguana lives on Anegada Island in the British Virgin Islands. The average length is thought to be a little less than 4 feet long.

CYCLURA RICORDI—RICORD'S ROCK IGUANA This iguana is found on the island of Hispaniola. It is the only place in the world where an island supports two distinct species of the same iguana. It is a somewhat shorter version of its island mate.

There are three more *Cyclura* species, all from the Exuma Cays of the Bahama islands. All are extremely threatened and grow to be less than 2 feet in length. They are the *Cyclura rileyi cristata*—Sandy Cay rock iguana; *Cyclura rileyi nuchallis*—Crooked-Acklins Island rock iguana; and *Cyclura rileyi rileyi*—San Salvador rock iguana.

DIPSOSAURUS DORSALIS

This species, commonly known as the desert iguana, is generally shorter than the popular *Iguana iguana*. Found mostly in the southwestern United States and Mexico, it is a desert dweller. There are many state laws that prohibit the capture of wild desert iguanas, and most of the ones that are for sale to the common hobbyist are captive-bred by experts.

IGUANA IGUANA—GREEN IGUANA This is the most commonly kept house pet in all of the Iguanidae family. This group is not in danger according to CITES. Although it is found from as far south as Brazil to as far north as Mexico and areas of the United States, the green iguanas sold as pets are bred on "farms" in Florida and Texas and Central America.

IGUANA DELICATISSIMA— ANTILLEAN GREEN IGUANA

While it is not yet officially a threatened species, this particular animal is losing the battle to remain in its natural habitat. Found on several islands off the Lesser Antilles, the Antillean green iguana is slightly smaller in size than the green iguana. The *Iguana delicatissima* also lacks the large subtympanal scales of the green iguana.

SAUROMALUS OBESUS

The Chuckwalla is the most easily identifiable of all iguanae; it looks like a fattened version of *Iguana iguana.* A native of the South-western American deserts, the Chuckwalla uses its most recognizable attribute to its advantage in the wild. When confronted by an aggressor, the Chuckwalla climbs into the narrowest of cracks and fattens itself up, lodging itself into the rocks so that it cannot be pulled out.

Its large back is also good for soaking up the sun's rays. Its tail also tends to be wider, thicker and shorter than that of its cousins. There are eleven varieties of *Sauromalus:*

SAUROMALUS ATER ATER This species is found from northern California to the Gulf of California.

SAUROMALUS ATER KLAUBERI These iguanas are found from Santa Catalina Island down in the Gulf of California.

SAUROMALUS ATER SHAWI— CHUCKWALLA These animals are found from the Isla San Marcos, from the Mexican Gulf of California.

SAUROMALUS AUSTRALIS This species is from the Baja region.

SAUROMALUS HISPIDUS This species is generally found on the Isla Angel de la Guarda and a few other islands.

SAUROMALUS OBESUS MULTI-FORMINATUS—GLENN CANYON CHUCKWALLA This species is generally found along the Colorado River canyon from Utah to Arizona.

SAUROMALUS OBESUS OBESUS—WESTERN CHUCKWALLA   This species is probably the most common member of the Sauromalus family. It is easily found almost anywhere in the southern United States.

SAUROMALUS OBESUS TOWNSENDI—SONORAN DESERT CHUCKWALLA   This species is generally found in Sonora, Mexico, and a few islands off its coast.

SAUROMALUS OBESUS TUMIDUS—ARIZONA CHUCKWALLA   Easily found throughout the Arizona and neighboring Mexican countryside.

SAUROMALUS SLEVENI—CHUCKWALLA   This species is from the Islas Carmen, Coronados and Monserrate. It is extremely rare and very threatened.

SAUROMALUS VARIUS—SAN ESTEBAN CHUCKWALLA OR PAINTED CHUCKWALLA   This iguana comes from the islands of San Esteban, Lobos and Pelicanos in the Gulf of California. Measuring more than 2 feet in length, this is the largest of the Chuckwallas. This species is also endangered.

CHAPTER ELEVEN

Resources

BOOKS

Bartlett, R. D., and Patricia P. Bartlett. *Iguanas.* Hauppage, NY: Barron's, 1995.

Burghardt, G. M., and A. S. Rand, eds. *Iguanas of the World.* Park Ridge, NJ: Noyes, 1982.

Coborn, John. *Caring for Green Iguanas.* Neptune, NJ: TFH, 1994.

de Vosjoli, Phillipe. *The Green Iguana Manual.* Lakeside, CA: Advanced Vivarium Systems, 1991.

Frye, Fredrick L., DVM., and W. Townsend. *Iguanas: A Guide to Their Biology and Captive Care.* Malabar, FL: Krieger, 1993.

Klingenberg, R. *Understanding Reptile Parasites.* Lakeside, CA: Advanced Vivarium Systems, 1991.

Mader, Douglas R. *Reptile Medicine and Surgery.* Philadelphia, PA: W. B. Saunders, 1996.

Moenich, David R. *Lizards.* Neptune, NJ: TFH, 1990.

Samuelson, Phillip, and Margaret A. Wissman, DVM. *Green Iguanas: An Owner's Guide.* Mission Viejo, CA: Bowtie Press, 1995.

MAGAZINES

Reptiles. Fancy Publications, Inc. 3 Burroughs, Irvine, CA 92718. (714) 855-8822.

Reptiles USA (annual). Fancy Publications, Inc. 3 Burroughs, Irvine, CA 92718. (714) 855-8822.

Vivarium. Journal of the American Federation of Herpetoculturists. P.O. Box 300067, Escondido, CA 92030-0067. (619) 747-4948.

INTERNET RESOURCES

Association of Reptile and Amphibian Veterinarians – www.arav.org

Giant Green Iguana Information Collection – www.sonic.net/ ~melissk/ig_fram.html

The Iguanas Mailing List – An on-line question and answer forum. http://iml.retina.net

The Iguana Pages – Information and links. www.baskingspot.com/iguanas

International Reptilian Online – On-line magazine. www.reptilian.co.uk

NATIONAL ORGANIZATIONS

International Iguana Society
Rte. 3, Box 328
Big Pine Key, FL 33043

American Federation of
Herpetoculturists
P.O. Box 300067
Escondido, CA 92030-0067
(Publishes *The Vivarium*)

National Herpetological Alliance
P.O. Box 5143
Chicago, IL 60680-5143

Society for the Study of Amphibians
and Reptiles
P.O. Box 626
Hays, KA 67601-0626

THERMOREGULATORY, FULL SPECTRUM LIGHTING, HEATING AND REPTILE EGG INCUBATION EQUIPMENT

Black Jungle Terrarium Supply
P.O. Box 93895
Las Vegas, NV 89193
(702) 242-0220

Energy Savers Unlimited, Inc.
http://www.esuweb.com

Helix Controls
12225 World Trade Drive (Suite C)
San Diego, CA 92128
(619) 674-7480
http://www.herp.com/helix/helix.html

J.S. Technologies
Habi-Temp
P.O. Box 12420
La Crescenta, CA 91224
(818) 353-1577
E-mail: jstech@earthlink.net

Kane Reptile Heat Mats
P.O. Box 774
Des Moines, IA 50303
(515) 262-3001
E-mail: kanemfg@worldnet.att.net

Lyon Electric Co. Inc.
Reptile Incubation Systems
2765 Main St.
Chula Vista, CA 91911
(619) 585-9900

Pro Products
36 Split Rock Rd.
Mahopac, NY 10541
(914) 628-8960
http://www.pro-products.com

Randall Burkey Co., Inc.
Incubators
117 Industrial Dr.
Boerne, TX 78006
(800) 531-1097

Reptronics
170 Creek Rd.
Bangor, PA 18013
(610) 588-6011

Vita-Lite
c/o Duro-Lite Lamps
9 Law Dr.
Fairfield, NJ 07004
(888) 738-8482

ZooMed Laboratories, Inc.
3199 McMillan
San Luis Obispo, CA 93401
(805) 542-9988
E-mail: zoomed@zoomed.com
http://www.zoomed.com

Put a picture of your iguana
in this box

Your Iguana's Name

Identifying Features ______________________

____

Date of Birth ______________________

Your Iguana's Veterinarian ______________________

Address ______________________

Phone Number ______________________

Medications ______________________

Vet Emergency Number ______________________

Additional Emergency Numbers ______________________

Favorite Foods ______________________

____

Tear me out!

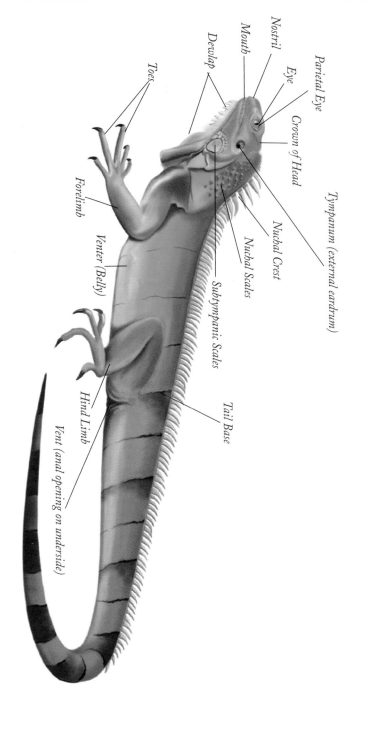

Parietal Eye

Nostril

Eye

Mouth

Crown of Head

Dewlap

Tympanum (external eardrum)

Toes

Nuchal Crest

Nuchal Scales

Forelimb

Subtympanic Scales

Venter (Belly)

Tail Base

Hind Limb

Vent (anal opening on underside)